THE CALIFORNIA DIRECTORY OF

FINE WINERIES

THIRD EDITION

THE CALIFORNIA DIRECTORY OF
FineWineries

K. Reka Badger, Cheryl Crabtree, and Daniel Mangin, Writers

Robert Holmes, Photographer

Tom Silberkleit, Editor and Publisher

WINE HOUSE PRESS

CONTENTS

INTRODUCTION 11

WHAT IS AN APPELLATION? 12

THE MAKING OF WINE 13

THE ART OF BARREL MAKING 14

MODERN STOPPERS 16

THE FOOD AND WINE CONNECTION 17

READING A WINE LABEL 18

THE ETIQUETTE OF WINE TASTING 19

SANTA BARBARA COUNTY WINERIES 23

Alma Rosa Winery & Vineyards

Beckmen Vineyards

Blair Fox Cellars

Byron

Cambria Estate Winery

Carhartt Vineyard

Carr Vineyards & Winery

Costa de Oro Winery

D'Alfonso-Curran Wines

Demetria Estate Winery

Fess Parker Winery & Vineyard

Foley Estates Vineyard & Winery

Foley Food & Wine Society

Foxen

Grassini Family Vineyards

Hitching Post Wines

Loring/Cargasacchi Tasting Room

Pali Wine Co.

Sanford Winery & Vineyards

Silver Wines

Zaca Mesa Winery & Vineyards

SAN LUIS OBISPO COUNTY WINERIES 71

Barr Estate Winery

Calcareous Vineyard

Caliza Winery

Castoro Cellars

Chamisal Vineyards

Derby Wine Estates

Eberle Winery

Eos

Grey Wolf Cellars and Barton
   Vineyards

Halter Ranch Vineyard

HammerSky Vineyards

Hearst Ranch Winery

Hearthstone Estate

J. Lohr Vineyards & Wines

Justin Vineyards & Winery

Laetitia Vineyard & Winery

Opolo Vineyards

PasoPort Wine Company

Pear Valley Vineyards

Penman Springs Vineyard

Pomar Junction Vineyard & Winery

Sextant Wines

Siot and Rotta Winery

SummerWood Winery

Talley Vineyards

Treana and Hope Family Wines

Vina Robles

Wild Horse Winery

Windward Vineyard

CENTRAL COAST WINE VARIETALS 136

ACKNOWLEDGMENTS 143

INTRODUCTION

Navigating California's burgeoning Central Coast wine country can be intimidating. Hundreds of wineries—from enchanting estates to storefront tasting rooms, from nationally recognized labels to hidden gems—can be found throughout the counties of Santa Barbara and San Luis Obispo. They are waiting to be discovered. The challenge is in deciding where to go and how to plan a trip. This book will be your indispensable traveling companion.

The fifty wineries in this fully updated, third edition of *The California Directory of Fine Wineries, Central Coast*, are known for producing some of the region's most admired wines. From the moment you walk into these wineries and tasting rooms, you will be invited to converse and sample at a leisurely tempo. In this down-to-earth wine country, passionate vineyard owners and winemakers enjoy experimenting and strive to make distinctive wines that please themselves as well as their devoted customers. Whether you are a novice wine taster or a longtime connoisseur, I suggest that you try unfamiliar wines. You'll be rewarded with outstanding blends and local specialties often unavailable elsewhere.

Although the quality of the winemaker's art is of paramount importance, the wineries are also notable as tourist destinations. Many feature distinctive contemporary architecture. Others are housed in meticulously preserved historic structures. Some host food-and-wine pairings, barrel tastings, art exhibits, concerts, grape stomps, and weekend barbecues. You will also enjoy taking informative behind-the-scenes tours, strolling through colorful gardens, and picnicking on the edge of the vineyards.

As you explore this region, you'll encounter some of California's most appealing scenery and attractions—mountain ranges, dramatic coastline, abundant parkland, and historic towns. Use the information in this book to plan your trip, and be sure to stop along the way to take in the sights. You have my promise that traveling to your destination will be as pleasurable as the wine tasted upon your welcome.

—Tom Silberkleit
Editor and Publisher
Wine House Press
Sonoma, California

What Is an Appellation?

Winemakers often showcase the source of their fruit by citing an *appellation* to describe the area where the wine grapes were grown. An appellation is a specific region that, in the United States, was traditionally determined by political borders such as state and county lines. Examples are California, Santa Barbara County, and San Luis Obispo County. In 1981 the Bureau of Alcohol, Tobacco, and Firearms, now the U.S. Alcohol and Tobacco Tax and Trade Bureau (TTB), initiated a system of American Viticultural Areas (AVAs) whose borders are based on climate and geography. Pre-existing politically defined appellations were grandfathered into the new system of AVAs. In 1985 federal regulators approved the massive Central Coast AVA, which embraces ten Pacific Coast counties, including San Luis Obispo and Santa Barbara counties. Using the name of either an appellation or an AVA on a label requires that a certain percentage of the wine in the bottle (75 and 85 percent, respectively) be made from grapes grown within the designation.

AVAs, in contrast to appellations, are defined by such natural features as soil types, prevailing winds, rivers, and mountain ranges. Wineries or other interested parties hoping to create an AVA must submit documented research to the TTB proving that the area's specific attributes clearly distinguish it from the surrounding region. The TTB has the authority to approve or deny the petition.

Winemakers know that identifying the origin of their grapes can lend prestige to a wine, particularly if the appellation has earned a reputation for quality. It also provides information about what's inside the bottle. For instance, a Pinot Noir from the hundred-square-mile Santa Rita Hills AVA (abbreviated Sta. Rita Hills to distinguish it from a similarly named appellation in Chile) is likely to vary significantly from one sourced from the California appellation, which includes grapes from all over the state. Moreover, informed consumers know that a Chardonnay from the Santa Maria Valley, for example, is apt to differ in both aroma and taste from a Chardonnay originating in Paso Robles. When a winery uses grapes from an off-site appellation to make a particular wine, the label indicates the source of the fruit, rather than the physical location of the winery. For instance, Sextant Wines, in the Paso Robles AVA, sources Chardonnay from its vineyard in Edna Valley. Hence the label reads "Sextant, Edna Valley Estate Chardonnay."

Santa Barbara and San Luis Obispo counties currently contain the following AVAs:

Santa Barbara County	San Luis Obispo County
Ballard Canyon	Arroyo Grande Valley
Happy Canyon of Santa Barbara	Edna Valley
Santa Maria Valley	Paso Robles
Santa Ynez Valley	Santa Maria Valley
Sta. Rita Hills	York Mountain

Proposed AVAs include Los Alamos region, Los Olivos District, and Santa Maria Bench.

THE MAKING OF WINE

Most vintners agree that wine is made not in the cellar, but in the vineyard, where sun, soil, and water — collectively known as *terroir* — influence varietal flavor. Growers select vineyard sites for many reasons, including exposure and low fertility, because lean soils often produce the most flavorful fruit. Based on the *terroir*, they plant varietals and clones (also called subvarietals) that will grow best, and then wait three years or longer for the vines to mature before ever picking a grape.

Harvest brings intense activity, as truckloads of ripe grapes roll into the winery, ready to be crushed and destemmed. After crush, white grapes are pressed, and their juice sent to barrels or stainless steel tanks for fermentation, while red grapes are fermented with skins and seeds to provide additional color and flavor. Winemakers introduce commercially grown yeast or sometimes rely on ambient wild yeast to trigger fermentation, a roiling process during which yeast converts grape sugar into alcohol and carbon dioxide. Fermentation stops when the yeast runs out of sugar, which results in a dry wine. Conversely, the winemaker may quickly chill the wine, killing the yeast and leaving behind a little residual sugar for sweetness.

After fermentation, many wines spend from a few months to a year or more in oak barrels where they develop complexity and absorb hints of the toasted interior of the barrel itself. Red wines usually rest in the barrel longer than whites. Most rosés and crisp white wines, such as Riesling, spend little or no time in barrels.

Throughout the process, winemakers taste their young wares, checking for signs of spoilage and imbalance. They analyze samples in a laboratory to determine the chemical makeup of the wine, which helps them to correct potential problems and maintain stability as the wines continue to evolve. Prior to bottling, vintners spend hours tasting wine from tanks and barrels to create optimum combinations for their final blends. Once in the bottle, rosés and light, fruity whites are usually released within a few months. Robust reds remain at the winery for several months to a year or so, which gives them a chance to mature and soften before their release.

To make sparkling wine using the *méthode champenoise*, vintners combine a blended base wine — usually Chardonnay or Pinot Noir fermented without the skins — with sugar and yeast. The mixture goes into heavy glass bottles, where a secondary fermentation takes place, giving the wine its signature bubbles. The wine ages for a year or more, and then dead yeast cells are removed in a process called disgorging, a little wine is added back to the bottle, and a natural cork is wired in place.

Wine lovers often buy several bottles of a favorite vintage and store them in a cellar or cool closet. That way, they can open a bottle every year or so, and enjoy the subtle flavor shifts as the wine continues to mature over time.

THE ART OF BARREL MAKING

Since ancient times, skilled artisans, called coopers, have made an array of casks for many purposes, including storage and shipping. Dry casks, often crafted of pine and cedar, held tobacco, flour, and other dry goods. A barrel is a cask designed to hold liquids, including wine. Handmade barrels reflect the highest form of the art of cooperage.

Until recent decades, French oak prevailed as the best type of wood for wine storage. During the Napoleonic era, the French planted a number of oak forests to supply the shipbuilding industry. Each forest produced trees with divergent character traits, and barrels made of wood from certain forests had distinct effects on the wine stored within them. In the early years of the U.S. wine industry, American oak seemed to overpower wine flavor. However, research determined that the strong influence came from the way people were preparing the wood and building the barrels. Today many wineries use American oak barrels, which are typically more affordable than their French counterparts. Some wineries also seek out Hungarian oak barrels, which yield distinctive flavors at a lower price point than French and American.

Barrel making begins with experts choosing high-quality wood by looking at tree shapes, growing conditions, and wood grain, as well as the presence of tannins, compounds that influence the flavor of wine. The best wood usually comes from older trees, more than a hundred years of age and at least five feet in diameter. Ideal wood should be straight and have no knots or burrs, and only traces of sap and regular rings. Workers split the logs into staves by hand, to avoid damage to veins in the wood grain, which could cause leakage in barrels. Then they plane the staves and store them outdoors in tiers for about three years to age naturally in wet and dry weather. This allows the wood to mellow out elements that could overpower the wine, such as tannins, scents, and impurities. Winemakers often choose barrels made of tough, porous white oak, which usually matures well in these conditions. When the staves are ready, they are cut and prepared for the cooper.

Barrels take about eight hours to complete. The cooper begins by "raising the barrel"—he takes premium staves and places them in a jig, a metal hoop that holds the staves fast. He pushes three hoops into place and waters the staves, then "toasts" them on a fire to the desired type to suit the wine grape and style: typically light, medium, or heavy. Lightly toasted barrels impart more oak flavor, while heavily toasted barrels give wines a charred or "roasted" aroma and smoky, spicy notes. The heat and moisture make the staves flexible enough for the cooper to take a winch and bend the staves into a barrel shape, tie them with trusses, and place the remaining iron or metal hoops around them. He carves a croze, or groove, in the ends to hold the flat, round barrel ends. Then he seals the ends with a dowel and river reed and finishes the barrel with mallet, plane, and sandpaper.

Barrels are heavy—they weigh up to 140 pounds when empty and much more when filled with wine. But the cylindrical shape allows workers to roll and turn barrels for easy transport. Winemakers use each barrel for about five to seven years. At that point, the porous wood fibers have absorbed as much wine as they can tolerate. They also have little flavor left to convey to the wine stored within. Thereafter, many barrels continue to contribute to winery life as planters, furniture, and wine-themed artistic creations.

MODERN STOPPERS:
CORK, PLASTIC, AND SCREWCAPS

It's an ancient question: What is the best way to close a wine bottle? Since the late 1600s, vintners have largely chosen stoppers made from cork tree bark. These time-tested closures usually provide an effective seal, potentially lasting as long as thirty years or more. At the same time, they are elastic and compressible, which allows for easy extraction. Many wine aficionados associate cork stoppers with a hallowed ritual, using corkscrews or other devices to remove the cork and launch the wine appreciation experience.

Corks, however, are not perfect stoppers. In past years, statistics estimated that nearly 20 percent of wine bottles were damaged by cork taint." This results from natural unnatural chemical compounds sources, for example, pesticides compounds contaminate the chemicals that give the wine corks occasionally disintegrate corks fail by allowing too much  problems, chiefly from "cork airborne fungi meeting up with (pollutants from industrial and wood preservatives). The cork bark and produce other a musty odor. Contaminated and crumble in the bottle. Some oxygen to pass through to the wine. Cork advocates claim that recent research has reduced the risk of cork taint to as little as 1 percent. Any risk at all is unacceptable to some winemakers, who now rely on other types of bottle stoppers.

Screwcaps, once associated with inexpensive, mass-produced wines, have grown increasingly popular in many countries around the world. The caps hold in place a seal liner, designed to allow a microscopic amount of breathability for aging wines over time. Screwcaps are easy to remove—all you need is an opposable thumb—and screwcap advocates say that even a monkey can open a bottle. More and more wineries are using screwcaps with great success, virtually eliminating the occurrence of damaged wine due to closure problems.

Synthetic (plastic) stoppers also offer a reliable sealing solution. They act in the same manner as corks and are removed from bottles with corkscrews, pulls, and other devices. Synthetic corks can provide an excellent seal. However, they are not as flexible as cork, and a highly effective seal makes them difficult to remove from the bottle. They are thus designed to oxidize and lose their elasticity within a few years and are not good candidates for long-term storage in wine cellars. These stoppers are best used for wines consumed upon release or soon thereafter.

Choice of stoppers also involves environmental considerations. The western Mediterranean region contains 6.6 million acres of cork oak tree (*Quercus suber*) forests. Bark from mature trees is harvested in environmentally friendly fashion every nine years, and trees typically live from 150 to 200 years. Cork stoppers are natural, renewable, recyclable, and biodegradable. The forests support wildlife habitats, absorb carbon dioxide from the atmosphere, and sustain local workers. Plastic can be recycled, but it is not made from environmentally friendly material and is not a sustainable product. Screwcaps are recyclable, but the manufacturing process requires much energy usage and releases greenhouses gases into the atmosphere.

As the stopper debate continues to rock the wine world, some wineries are returning to a simple, environmentally friendly solution used for centuries. They sell whole barrels directly to restaurants and tasting rooms, which offer "barrel wines" on tap to customers—no stoppers, bottles, or packaging at all.

THE FOOD AND WINE CONNECTION

The Central Coast boasts cultural and lifestyle advantages associated with urban centers, yet remains at heart an agricultural region. In Santa Barbara and San Luis Obispo counties, more than 50 percent of the combined acreage supports livestock and food crops. Local farmers supply markets and restaurants with such Central Coast specialties as avocados, strawberries, heritage apples, and heirloom tomatoes. Ranchers provide fresh eggs, sausage, and grass-fed beef, lamb, pork, buffalo, venison, and chicken. Along the coast, shellfish wranglers tend briny beds of abalone and oysters, and hard-working fishermen bring in fresh seafood daily. Area purveyors supplement the bounty with crusty breads and baked goods, extra-virgin olive oils, and artisanal cheeses.

Most of the region's edible delights can be found at farmers' markets taking place every day somewhere on the Central Coast. One of the largest in California is held every Thursday night in downtown San Luis Obispo. Part open-air market, part street fair, it features more than 120 vendors tending tables brimming with seasonal produce, meats, honey, nuts, and cut flowers. Grill masters dish up sizzling sausage, ribs, and tri-tip sandwiches from aromatic barbecues, and musical groups play on just about every side street. Jugglers, unicyclists, puppeteers, and dancers lend a festive flavor to the popular market.

The Central Coast's agricultural wealth, along with its dynamic culture, attracts world-class chefs and drives culinary innovation. Encouraged by supportive communities, these chefs riff on the cuisines of Asia, Latin America, Europe, and the Mediterranean countries. They dish up distinctly local fare, too, including Santa Maria–style barbecue, based on the mid-nineteenth-century feasts served by cattlemen during roundups and fiestas. The centerpiece of the meal is grilled beef: either top-block or tri-tip, a triangular cut of sirloin traditionally ground into hamburger. It is served with salsa, small savory pink beans called *pinquitos,* green salad, and garlic bread. In the mid-1950s, a Santa Maria–area butcher grilled a tri-tip as an experiment, gave away juicy slices to customers, and ignited a food trend. Today, the beef is rubbed with a mixture of garlic, salt, and pepper and cooked slowly over a glowing red oak fire.

Naturally, contemporary chefs often pair their creations with local wines. Winemaking began on the Central Coast in 1782 when Franciscan missionaries planted grapevines near the city of Santa Barbara. By the turn of the twenty-first century, Santa Barbara and San Luis Obispo counties were home to more than 50,000 vineyard acres supporting fifty-five different varieties of wine grapes. The counties' three-hundred-plus wineries produce an astonishing array of wines, including Rhône-, Burgundy-, and Bordeaux-style offerings; Cal-Italian blends; and distinctly regional wines.

Home to bustling cities and two renowned universities, the Central Coast offers the benefits of urban life in a wonderfully pastoral environment. With their fertile fields, magnificent coastline, and thriving vinicultural scene, Santa Barbara and San Luis Obispo counties provide all the elements for a perfect connection of food and wine.

READING A WINE LABEL

When you encounter an unfamiliar bottle of wine, you can learn a lot about it from inspecting the label. Federal law requires wineries to print specific information on the front label of each bottle. Some wineries include details on how a wine was made or how well it will pair with specific foods, usually on a separate label on the back of the bottle.

Most prominently displayed on the label is the name of the winery or the brand name. Also given emphasis is the type of wine. In most cases, this is the grape varietal, such as Chardonnay or Zinfandel. To carry the name of a varietal, the wine must be made of 75 percent of that varietal. Wineries can also use a generic name or a proprietary one such as Halter Ranch Vineyard's Ancestor Estate Reserve.

The place of origin on the label tells you where the grapes were grown, not necessarily where the wine was made. A label bearing the name "California" means that 100 percent of the grapes were grown within the state. To use a county name, 75 percent of the grapes must come from that county. To use an American Viticultural Area (AVA) or appellation, at least 85 percent of the grapes must come from the defined area. The vintage is the year the grapes were harvested, not the year the wine was released. The wine must contain at least 95 percent of the stated vintage. Labels sometimes identify an individual vineyard. This is a way for the winemaker to indicate that the grapes came from an exceptional source. To be a vineyard-designated wine, a minimum of 95 percent of the grapes must have come from the vineyard named. Any wine with an alcohol content of more than 14 percent must carry this information. Wines designated as "table wine," with 7 to 14 percent alcohol content, are not required to state such information. American-made wine that contains sulfites must say so on the front or back label. Sulfur dioxide is a natural by-product of winemaking. Some wineries also add sulfites as a preservative.

Other information found on labels may include the description "estate bottled." This tells you that the winery owns (or controls) the vineyard where the grapes were grown and that both the winery and the vineyard are in the same AVA. A bottle labeled "reserve" indicates that the wine is of a superior quality compared with the winery's nonreserve offerings.

Labels for sparkling wines may contain the term *méthode champenoise.* The most salient feature of this process is allowing the wine to ferment for a second time inside the bottle, resulting in bubbles that are finer than those in sparkling wine made by other methods. Vintage sparkling wines are designated as either regular vintage or *prestige cuvée* (also called *tête de cuvée* or premium vintage), meaning that the wine is the top of the line.

THE ETIQUETTE OF WINE TASTING

Most of the wineries profiled in this book offer amenities ranging from inviting gardens to winemaker dinners, but their main attraction is the tasting room. This is where winery employees get a chance to share their products and knowledge with consumers, in hopes of establishing a lifelong relationship. They are there to please.

Yet, for some visitors, the ritual of tasting fine wines can be intimidating. Perhaps it's because swirling wine and using a spit bucket seem to be unnatural acts. But with a few tips, even a first-time taster can enjoy the experience.

After all, the point of tasting is to enhance your knowledge by learning the differences among varieties of wines, styles of winemaking, and appellations. A list of available wines is usually posted, beginning with whites and ending with the heaviest reds or, if available, dessert wines. Look for the tasting notes, which are typically set out on the counter; refer to them as you taste each wine.

After you are served, hold the stem of the glass with your thumb and as many fingers as you need to maintain control. Lift the glass up to the light and note the color and intensity of the wine. Good wines tend to be bright, with the color fading near the rim. Next, gently swirl the wine in the glass. Observe how much of the wine adheres to the sides of the glass. If lines — called legs — are visible, the wine is viscous, indicating body or weight as well as a high alcohol content. Now, tip the glass to about a 45-degree angle, take a short sniff, and concentrate on the aromas. Swirl the wine again to aerate it, releasing additional aromas. Take another sniff and see if the "bouquet" reminds you of anything — rose petals, citrus fruit, or a freshly ironed pillowcase, for example — that will help you identify the aroma.

Finally, take a sip and swirl the wine around your tongue, letting your taste buds pick up all the flavors. The wine may remind you of honey or cherries or mint — as with the "nosing," try to make as many associations as you can. Then spit the wine into the bucket on the counter. Afterward, notice how long the flavor stays in your mouth; a long finish is the ideal. If you don't want another taste, just pour the wine remaining in your glass into the bucket and move on. Remember, the more you spit or pour out, the more wines you can sample.

The next level of wine tasting involves guided tastings and food-and-wine pairings. In these sessions, a few cheeses or appetizers are paired with a flight of wines, usually a selection of three red or three white wines presented in the recommended order of tasting. The server will explain what goes with what.

If you still feel self-conscious, practice at home. Once you are in a real tasting room, you'll be better able to focus on the wine itself. That's the real payoff, because once you learn what you like and why you like it, you'll be able to recognize wines in a similar vein anywhere in the world.

SANTA BARBARA COUNTY

One of the world's extraordinary geographic anomalies defines Santa Barbara County wine country. Rather than being oriented north-south, the mountain ranges run east-west. The towering peaks and sloping hillsides funnel cool winds and fog from the Pacific Ocean through river valleys, resulting in an incredible geographic diversity and a superior environment for growing premium wine grapes.

Until the late 1960s, only a handful of vineyards existed here. After University of California scientific research pointed to the area's potential as a premier wine-grape region, pioneering vintners planted vines with little other than instinct to guide them. Their experiences and successes—especially with award-winning Pinot Noir and Chardonnay—helped put Santa Barbara County on the international wine map. Today the county boasts more than 23,000 acres of vineyards. Of the county's many wineries, more than half produce fewer than 2,000 cases a year.

Vineyards, interspersed with organic farms, thoroughbred horse ranches, and cattle ranches, blanket the rural landscape north of the Santa Ynez Mountains. Two-lane roads connect the small Danish-themed town of Solvang with the Old West villages of Los Olivos and Santa Ynez, and picturesque Highway 246 winds westward through Buellton and the Santa Rita Hills to the westernmost city of Lompoc. These uncrowded roads attract cycling enthusiasts from around the world, who enjoy pedaling for miles in a stunning pastoral setting. They also come to train and compete in major international races such as the annual Tour of California. The vast Los Padres National Forest bounds the eastern sectors. On the south side, the wild beaches of the rugged Gaviota coast stretch forty miles to the vibrant city of Santa Barbara.

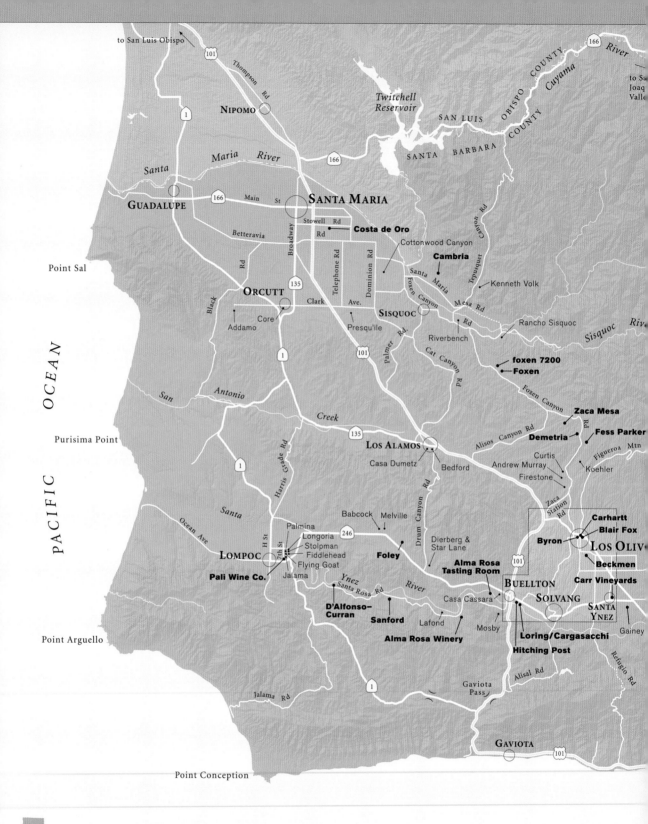

SANTA BARBARA
COUNTY WINERIES

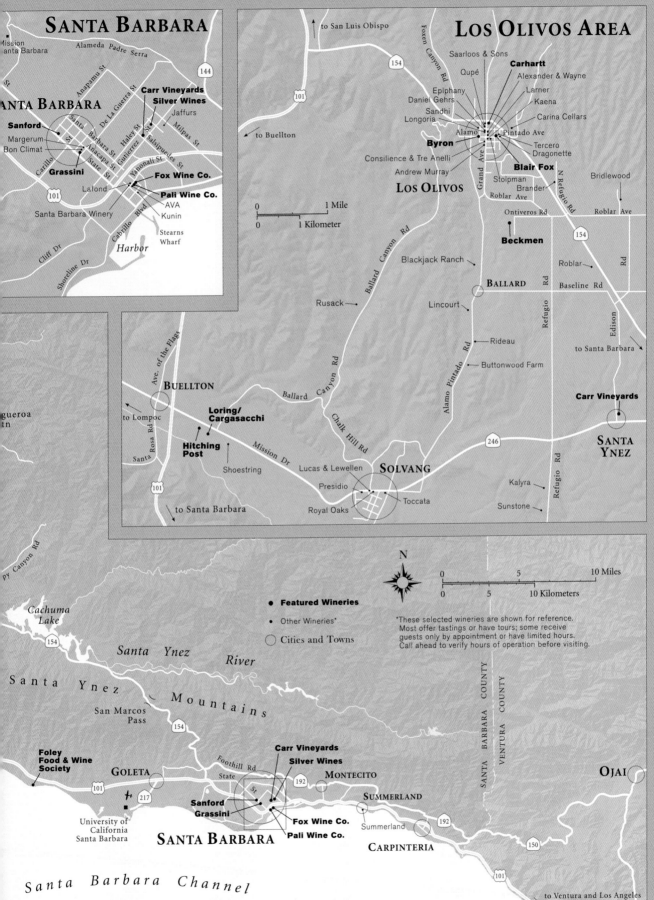

SANTA BARBARA

SANTA BARBARA

to San Luis Obispo

LOS OLIVOS AREA

SANTA BARBARA

Mission Santa Barbara

Alameda Padre Serra

144

Anapamu St

De La Guerra St

Haley St

Milpas St

Jaffurs

Carr Vineyards
Silver Wines

Sanford

Margerum
Bon Climat

Santa Barbara St

Anacapa St

Gutierrez St

Salsipuedes St

State St

Grassini

Carrillo St

Lafond

Yanonali St

Fox Wine Co.

Pali Wine Co.

AVA

Kunin

Santa Barbara Winery

Cabrillo Blvd

Stearns Wharf

Cliff Dr

Shoreline Dr

Harbor

101

0 ——— 1 Mile

0 ——— 1 Kilometer

to Buellton

Foxen Canyon Rd

154

101

Saarloos & Sons

Qupé

Carhartt

Alexander & Wayne

Epiphany

Larner

Daniel Gehrs

Kaena

Sandhi

Carina Cellars

Longoria

Alamo

Pintado Ave

Byron

Tercero

Dragonette

Consilience & Tre Anelli

Blair Fox

Andrew Murray

Stolpman

LOS OLIVOS

Brander

Grand Ave

Roblar Ave

N Refugio Rd

Bridlewood

Ontiveros Rd

Roblar Ave

Beckmen

154

Blackjack Ranch

Roblar

Rd

Refugio Rd

Baseline Rd

BALLARD

Rusack

Lincourt

Edison Rd

Rideau

to Santa Barbara

Ballard Canyon Rd

Buttonwood Farm

Alamo Pintado Rd

BUELLTON

Ave. of the Flags

to Lompoc

**Loring/
Cargasacchi**

Santa Rosa Rd

**Hitching
Post**

Shoestring

Ballard Canyon Rd

Chalk Hill Rd

Mission Dr

Lucas & Lewellen

SOLVANG

246

Carr Vineyards

**SANTA
YNEZ**

Presidio

Toccata

Kalyra

Royal Oaks

Sunstone

Refugio Rd

101

to Santa Barbara

Figueroa Mtn

Py Canyon Rd

*Cachuma
Lake*

N

0 ——— 5 ——— 10 Miles

0 ——— 5 ——— 10 Kilometers

154

• **Featured Wineries**

• Other Wineries*

○ Cities and Towns

*These selected wineries are shown for reference.
Most offer tastings or have tours; some receive
guests only by appointment or have limited hours.
Call ahead to verify hours of operation before visiting.

Santa Ynez River

S a n t a   Y n e z

M o u n t a i n s

San Marcos Pass

154

SANTA BARBARA COUNTY

VENTURA COUNTY

OJAI

**Foley
Food & Wine
Society**

GOLETA

101

217

Carr Vineyards
Silver Wines

Foothill Rd

State St

192

MONTECITO

Sanford
Grassini

University of
California
Santa Barbara

SANTA BARBARA

Fox Wine Co.
Pali Wine Co.

SUMMERLAND

Summerland

192

CARPINTERIA

150

Santa   Barbara   Channel

101

to Ventura and Los Angeles

ALMA ROSA WINERY & VINEYARDS

In the late 1960s, U.C. Berkeley geography graduate Richard Sanford returned from service in Vietnam yearning for a career far removed from the sadness of war. The prospect of growing Pinot Noir grapes intrigued him, and he embarked on a study of California climate data collected since 1900. The statistics revealed fascinating patterns in northern Santa Barbara County, where the unusual transverse mountain range runs east-west, funneling cool maritime air through the valleys to moderate the growing climate. Sanford was convinced that this part of the state could produce world-class Pinot Noir grapes to rival the best in France.

Sanford drove the roads in the hills and valleys near Lompoc with an agricultural thermometer attached to his windshield  and discovered temperature variations ideal for Pinot Noir in the Santa Rita Hills, where grape growing was virtually unheard of at the time. In 1970 he cofounded the region's first Pinot Noir vineyard, Sanford & Benedict. In 1981 Sanford and his wife, Thekla, started Sanford Winery and a year later purchased the seven-hundred-acre Rancho El Jabalí (Ranch of the Wild Boar). They planted the county's first certified organic vineyards and made balanced, elegant wines that garnered widespread international acclaim and helped establish Sta. Rita Hills as an official appellation.

In 2005 the Sanfords separated from their namesake winery and began a new venture, retaining Rancho El Jabalí. In Spanish, *alma* means "soul," and the name Alma Rosa embodies the Sanfords' philosophy that their wines reflect the soul of the historic rancho. Alma Rosa focuses on continuing the Sanfords' reputation for excellence in Pinot Noir and Chardonnay, as well as small quantities of Pinot Gris, Pinot Blanc, and Pinot Noir Vin Gris, a dry rosé. Alma Rosa recently planted additional vines to expand the rancho's seven-acre El Jabalí Vineyard, and a new winery and tasting room are scheduled for completion in 2016. In the meantime, visitors can sample Alma Rosa wines at its new tasting facility on Buellton's Industrial Way. The neighborhood was originally a cluster of 16,000-square-foot bays used for storage or industrial uses. It is quickly evolving into an eclectic mix of wineries and tasting rooms, breweries, a distillery, restaurants, and high-tech firms. Designed by local architect Ken Radtkey, the tasting room has large skylights and a full-grown tree as a centerpiece. Guests can connect with Rancho El Jabalí's soul through the character-rich wines and vivid vineyard images on display.

ALMA ROSA WINERY & VINEYARDS
7250 Santa Rosa Rd.
Buellton, CA 93427

TASTING ROOM:
181 #C Industrial Way
Buellton, CA 93427
805-688-9090
info@almarosawinery.com
almarosawinery.com

FOUNDERS: Richard and Thekla Sanford.

LOCATION: Several blocks west of U.S. 101, off Hwy. 246 West.

APPELLATION: Sta. Rita Hills.

HOURS: 11 A.M.–4:30 P.M. daily.

TASTINGS: $10 or $15 for 4 wines. Reservations required for groups of 6 or more.

TOURS: Of the vineyard, by appointment.

THE WINES: Chardonnay, Pinot Blanc, Pinot Gris, Pinot Noir, Pinot Noir–Vin Gris.

SPECIALTIES: Chardonnay, Pinot Noir.

CELLAR MASTER: Richard Sanford.

ANNUAL PRODUCTION: 12,000 cases.

OF SPECIAL NOTE: Vineyard tours offer private access to El Jabalí's beautiful setting with groves of sycamore and redwoods, birds and other wildlife, and a spring-fed creek. Special bottlings sometimes available in tasting room.

NEARBY ATTRACTIONS: OstrichLand USA (33-acre ostrich ranch); Elverhøj Museum of History and Art (exhibits on Danish community in Solvang); Santa Barbara Soaring (glider rides); historic Mission Santa Inés; Wildling Art Museum (art of the American wilderness).

BECKMEN VINEYARDS

BECKMEN VINEYARDS
2670 Ontiveros Rd.
Los Olivos, CA 93441
805-688-8664
info@beckmenvineyards
.com
beckmenvineyards.com

OWNERS: Thomas and
Judith Beckmen.

LOCATION: 2 miles south of
flagpole in Los Olivos via
Grand Ave. and Roblar Ave.

APPELLATION: Santa Ynez
Valley.

HOURS: 11 A.M.–5 P.M. daily.

TASTINGS: $10 for 6 wines.
$15 for 6 reserve wines.

TOURS: None.

THE WINES: Cabernet Sauvi-
gnon, Counoise, Grenache,
Grenache Blanc, Marsanne,
Mourvèdre, Sauvignon
Blanc, Syrah, Viognier.

SPECIALTY: Purisima Mountain Vineyard–designated
wines.

WINEMAKER: Mikael Sigouin.

ANNUAL PRODUCTION:
16,000 cases.

OF SPECIAL NOTE: Two scenic
ponds and numerous pic-
nic areas (gazebos, tables,
decks). Pets and children
welcome. Small gift shop
with clothing, corkscrews
and other wine-related
items, oils, and vinegars.
Annual events include
Santa Barbara County
Vintner's Festival (April)
and Harvest Festival
(October). Most reserve
wines available only in
tasting room.

NEARBY ATTRACTIONS:
Historic buildings in
Los Olivos and Ballard;
Clairmont Farm Lavender
Company; Quicksilver
Miniature Horse Ranch.

A five-minute drive along peaceful country roads south of the quaint village of Los Olivos leads to the Beckmen Vineyards estate—one of the most idyllic tasting room settings in the Santa Ynez Valley. Rows of vines and serene landscaped grounds surround the tasting room and winery buildings, where every phase of winemaking, from crush to bottle, takes place. Covered gazebos line the shores of two shimmering ponds that provide lush habitat for migrating birds and other wildlife, oak and willow trees, and native plants.

The Beckmen family founded the estate twenty years ago, when only a handful of growers in the area were experimenting with Rhône varietals. Tom Beckmen had spent his childhood working on a ranch near Chicago and put himself through college by managing farm programs. In the early 1960s, Beckmen founded the Roland Corporation U.S., which pioneered electronic music and merged music and computer applications. Yearning to return to his farming roots, he sold Roland in 1993. He was certain that the Santa Ynez Valley had vast potential to produce world-class wines. He and his wife, Judith, bought an established forty-acre property and, along with son Steve, founded Beckmen Vineyards in 1994. Tom and Steve quickly began to revitalize the site. They removed the sixteen original acres of vines and planted carefully selected varietals, clones, and rootstocks.

In 1996 the family purchased a 365-acre ranch near Ballard Canyon that appeared to have ideal conditions for growing world-class Rhône varietals: high elevations, rare limestone subsoils, and unusual microclimates. They named the estate Purisima Mountain Vineyard and embarked on one of the most ambitious and meticulous hillside vineyard endeavors in the history of Santa Barbara County. Conceived as a "palette of small vineyards," the cultivated areas are individually tended in accordance with their unique needs. Purisima Mountain Vineyard now enjoys widespread acclaim for its elegant, complex, and character-rich fruit. Nearly 130 acres of the vineyard are farmed 100 percent biodynamically (officially certified in 2008). Steve Beckmen, winemaker Mikael Sigouin, and assistant winemaker Kyle Knapp work closely together to handcraft grapes from both estates into a diverse range of Rhône varietal wines. They also produce a popular Cuvée Le Bec blend and small quantities of Cabernet Sauvignon and Sauvignon Blanc.

Steve Beckmen and winemaker Mikael Sigouin are often in the tasting room, pouring wine and sharing their winemaking philosophy. Visitors can also sip wines at tables on the adjacent outdoor deck to enjoy expansive views of the estate vineyards, ponds, and wildlife areas.

BLAIR FOX CELLARS

The small town of Los Olivos looks much as it did in the late 1800s when the stagecoach stopped here to rest weary travelers and horses. A tall flagpole anchors the main intersection, and old Victorians and country cottages line the broad avenues. One such cottage, with rustic cedar siding, sits on a peaceful corner a short stroll from the flagpole. It houses a popular coffee shop, where locals gather to relax. It also holds the Blair Fox Cellars tasting room, where winemaker Blair Fox's limited-quantity, handcrafted Rhône wines take center stage.

Fox grew up in Santa Barbara and began pre-med studies at U.C. Santa Barbara. He transferred to U.C. Davis, where he took an enology class and found it so captivating that he switched career plans. Fox returned to Santa Barbara with a degree in viticulture and enology, and a newfound passion for Syrah, Viognier, and other Rhône varieties. After working at a small Santa Ynez winery for three years, Fox traveled through France's Rhône Valley and then worked as a winemaker in the McLaren Vale wine region in Australia. He returned to California in 2002, and Fess Parker Winery

hired him to oversee the Rhône wine production. In 2005 Fox became head winemaker of both Fess Parker Winery and its sister label, Epiphany. His talents quickly garnered him much praise and numerous accolades, including the coveted André Tchelistcheff Winemaker of the Year Award in 2008.

Fox still works at Fess Parker Winery, but crafts small-lot, vineyard-designated Syrah and other Rhône wines for his Blair Fox Cellars label. He sources most grapes from the all-organic, hand-farmed Fox Family Vineyard in Los Olivos, where vines thrive in ideal growing conditions: extreme hillsides with rocky, nutrient-poor soil. Fox literally affixes his "thumbprints" through all phases of production, from punchdowns, racking, and bottling to disgorging sparkling wines.

Fox shares the results of his creative techniques in the cottage tasting room, which feels much like the winemaker's family home. Eclectic furnishings and art contribute to the warm, welcoming vibe. Fox often hangs out to chat with visitors, as does his wife, Sarah, who helps with all facets of the business. In 2013 the family opened a second tasting room in downtown Santa Barbara's eclectic Funk Zone. It occupies a nook within the Santa Barbara Art Foundry, where visitors can watch molten brass turn into intricate sculptures. Tasting here centers around the approachable Fox Wine Co. line of Pinot Noir, Chardonnay, and Rhône varietal wines, which Blair and Sarah make together. Visitors can sample wines at the zinc-topped bar or at tables amid galleries filled with local and internationally renowned art.

BLAIR FOX CELLARS
2902-B San Marcos Ave.
Los Olivos, CA 93441
805-691-1678
info@blairfoxcellars.com
blairfoxcellars.com

FOX WINE CO.
120 Santa Barbara St.
Santa Barbara, CA 93101
805-699-6329
info@foxwineco.com
foxwineco.com

OWNERS: Blair and Sarah Fox.

LOCATION: Blair Fox Cellars: Front door is on Alamo Pintado Ave. Fox Wine Co.: Inside Santa Barbara Art Foundry.

APPELLATIONS: All within Santa Barbara County.

HOURS: Blair Fox Cellars: 12 P.M.–5 P.M. Friday– Sunday, and by appointment. Fox Wine Co.: 11 A.M.– 6 P.M. daily.

TASTINGS: Blair Fox Cellars: $12 for 5 wines. Fox Wine Co.: $10 for 5 wines, $15 for 5 wines plus 2 additional reserve wines.

TOURS: None.

THE WINES: Blair Fox Cellars: Grenache, Petite Sirah, Syrah, Vermentino, Viognier. Fox Wine Co.: Chardonnay, Pinot Noir, Sauvignon Blanc, Rhône varieties.

SPECIALTIES: Vineyard-designated Syrahs, estate-grown Grenache, Syrah, Petite Sirah, Vermentino.

WINEMAKER: Blair Fox.

ANNUAL PRODUCTION: Blair Fox Cellars: 1,000 cases. Fox Wine Co.: 1,000 cases.

OF SPECIAL NOTE: Estate vineyard is organically grown and farmed entirely by hand. Small, ultraboutique winery; wines available only in tasting room. Winemaker Blair Fox is often in the tasting room.

BYRON

BYRON
2367 Alamo Pintado Ave.
Los Olivos, CA 93441
805-938-7365
info@byronwines.com
byronwines.com

OWNER: Barbara Banke.

LOCATION: Downtown
Los Olivos.

APPELLATION: Santa Maria
Valley.

HOURS: 11 A.M.–5 P.M. daily.

TASTINGS: $10 for 5 wines.
$20 for 5 reserve wines.
Groups of 8 or more by
appointment.

TOURS: None.

THE WINES: Chardonnay,
Pinot Blanc, Pinot Noir.

SPECIALTIES: Estate-grown,
vineyard-designated Pinot
Noir and Chardonnay.

WINEMAKER:
Jonathan Nagy.

OF SPECIAL NOTE: Tasting
room is pet friendly. Open
house at the tasting room
for Santa Barbara County
Vintner's Festival (April)
and Harvest Festival (October). Pinot Blanc, six types
of Pinot Noir, single-clone
estate Chardonnay, and
GSM (Grenache, Syrah,
Mourvèdre) wines available
only in tasting room.

NEARBY ATTRACTIONS:
Historic buildings in
Los Olivos and Ballard;
Clairmont Farm Lavender
Company; Quicksilver
Miniature Horse Ranch.

In a 2010 video, Byron winemaker Jonathan Nagy says singer Barbara Mandrell's hit song "I Was Country When Country Wasn't Cool" aptly describes Byron, whose grape-growing roots date back more than half a century. The story begins in 1964 with the Nielson Vineyard, the first commercial planting in Santa Barbara County. Its *terroir* is the Santa Maria Bench, in the Santa Maria Valley, about twenty miles from the Pacific Ocean. The mountains in the north and south channel the fog and maritime winds eastward through the valley. These cooling influences, combined with mineral-rich soils, yield grapes packed with intense flavor, depth, and complexity.

Fast-forward to the early 1980s, when just a handful of vintners were growing Pinot Noir grapes in the county. After working at Zaca Mesa Winery, winemaker "Byron" Ken Brown knew that the bench held great promise for world-class Burgundian wine grapes. In 1984 he acquired the original Nielson Vineyard, founded Byron winery, and transformed the premium estate grapes into much-lauded wines that earned Byron a solid place on the international wine map. In 1991 Brown and the Byron team launched a series of trials, dubbed "The Big Experiment," to help determine which

vines fared best in particular subsites on the estate. They planted twenty-three clone and rootstock combinations of Pinot Noir along with several Chardonnay clones, then fermented each combination separately and measured the numbers, flavors, and style of wines produced from every block.

Barbara Banke, owner of neighboring Cambria Estate Winery, acquired Byron in 2007 and used the results of the experiment to guide a major replanting. More than four hundred acres (includ-ing the historic Nielson Vineyard) were broken into dozens of subsites, and rootstocks and clones (including nineteen of Pinot Noir) were matched to the subtleties of the *terroir*. Nagy, Byron's head winemaker since 2003, says the now mature vines provide him with an extraordinary array of flavors and textures to craft artisanal, small-lot wines. The Monument Pinot Noir, Byron's finest red wine, is a blend of the best barrels from the paramount blocks on the estate.

Byron celebrated its thirtieth anniversary in 2014. Four years earlier, the winery opened a tasting room in Los Olivos. A small set of brick steps leads to the contemporary space, where visitors sample wines and view historic photos, including those of the Nielson Vineyard in 1964.

CAMBRIA ESTATE WINERY

In the far northeast corner of Santa Barbara County, the Santa Maria Bench overlooks the ancient, gravelly banks of the Sisquoc River. The native Chumash called the area *tepuztli*, or "copper coin." Later, Spanish settlers called it Tepusquet (*tep*-us-kay). The steep slopes of the Tepusquet Mountains rise from the valley north of the bench, creating an unobstructed funnel for the cooling coastal breezes and fog that flow from the ocean seventeen miles to the west. In 1970 and 1971, pioneering Central Coast viticulturalist Louis Lucas and partners George Lucas and Alfred Gagnon planted Tepusquet Vineyard along this remarkable benchland, part of the 1838 Rancho Tepusquet Mexican land grant. The grapes thrived, and winemakers began to covet the fruit grown on the Santa Maria Bench for the rich, expressive character that the *terroir* imparts to cool-climate varieties such as Pinot Noir, Chardonnay, and Syrah.

In 1986 Barbara Banke, proprietor of several family-owned California wineries, purchased a portion of the original Tepusquet Vineyard. She established Cambria Estate Winery the next year to produce single-vineyard and small-block Chardonnays and Pinot Noirs, along with small quantities of Syrah and Viognier. Today Cambria Estate Winery occupies 1,600 southwest-facing acres and includes a winery, cellar, and tasting room. Banke named two of the four sustainably farmed estate vineyards after her daughters, Katherine and Julia; the other two are Tepusquet, in honor of the historic origins, and Bench Break, on the steepest slope above the estate.

Cambria has identified seventeen distinct soil types and many microclimates on the estate, and recently began replanting vineyard blocks to apply knowledge gained from more than two decades of experimentation. Many blocks are farmed and harvested individually according to their unique soils, microclimate, and elevation. Head winemaker Denise Shurtleff, who joined Cambria in 1999, crafts most of the handpicked estate grapes into nearly fifteen different bottlings. Pinot Noir grapes from Julia's Vineyard are sold to other wineries, including nearby Bonaccorsi, Foxen, and Hitching Post Wines.

A half-mile drive through the vineyards leads to Cambria's stone winery building. The tasting room, tucked in a corner on the top floor of the winery, was completely remodeled in 2006. Copper jugs and spittoons sit on a sleek, L-shaped brushed-concrete bar. An exhibit features photos of the barrel-making process. Glass windows enable visitors to observe winery operations in the barrel storage room below. Visitors can relax on the leather sofa before the fireplace and picnic on a nearby knoll with sweeping views of the Santa Maria Bench and Tepusquet Mountains.

CAMBRIA ESTATE WINERY
5475 Chardonnay Ln.
Santa Maria, CA 93454
805-938-7318
info@cambriawines.com
cambriawines.com

OWNER: Barbara Banke.

LOCATION: 12 miles east of downtown Santa Maria on the Foxen Trail.

APPELLATION: Santa Maria Valley.

HOURS: 10 A.M.–5 P.M. daily.

TASTINGS: $10 for 5 wines.

TOURS: By request.

THE WINES: Chardonnay, Pinot Gris, Pinot Noir, Syrah, Viognier.

SPECIALTIES: Estate-grown vineyard-designated Pinot Noirs and Chardonnays.

WINEMAKER:
Denise Shurtleff.

OF SPECIAL NOTE: Gift shop with books, clothing, and small selection of deli foods. Small patio with tables adjacent to tasting room. Picnic area on knoll overlooking vineyards. Single-clone estate Chardonnays and Pinot Noirs, Pinot Gris, and Syrah available only in tasting room.

NEARBY ATTRACTION:
Colson Canyon Road Mountain Bike and Hiking Trail.

CARHARTT VINEYARD

CARHARTT VINEYARD
2990-A Grand Ave.
Los Olivos, CA 93441
805-693-5100
info@carharttvineyard.com
carharttvineyard.com

OWNERS: Mike and Brooke
Carhartt.

LOCATION: Just under 100
yards from Hwy. 154.

APPELLATION: Santa Ynez
Valley.

HOURS: 11 A.M.–6 P.M. daily.

TASTINGS: $10 for 6 wines.

TOURS: None.

THE WINES: Merlot,
Pinot Noir, Sangiovese,
Sauvignon Blanc, Syrah,
Zinfandel.

SPECIALTIES: Estate Syrah,
Merlot, Sangiovese.

WINEMAKERS: Brooke, Mike,
and Chase Carhartt.

ANNUAL PRODUCTION:
4,500 cases.

OF SPECIAL NOTE: Small-
case production of up to
18 different wines. The
smallest tasting room in
the county. Winemakers
pour wine for guests.

NEARBY ATTRACTIONS:
Wildling Art Museum (art
of the American wilder-
ness); historic buildings
in Los Olivos and Ballard;
Clairmont Farm Lavender
Company; Quicksilver
Miniature Horse Ranch.

At the northern end of Grand Avenue, the main street in Los Olivos, sits an unassuming 1950s wooden cottage covered with climbing roses—the Carhartt Vineyard tasting room. Nearly everything here, indoors and out, reflects a sense of place—of deep connections to the land and people. Wooden tubs with flowers line the walkway and extend from the cottage down the block. On most days, owner Mike Carhartt welcomes visitors into the intimate space and, at the faux stone bar, proudly pours tastes of wines that he has handcrafted with his wife, Brooke, and son, Chase. Behind the cottage, Japanese maples and a neighbor's pepper tree shade a cozy patio and garden.

The Carhartt connection to the Santa Ynez Valley took root long ago. A descendant of Hamilton Carhartt, founder of the famed Carhartt Overall Company, Mike grew up on the family's historic Rancho Santa Ynez, a large cattle and horse ranch. In 1993 he and Brooke acquired fifty acres of the former family estate. Mike had been around farming all of his life and had watched the valley develop into a premier wine region, so it made perfect sense for him to devote a portion of the ranch to wine grapes. In 1996 he and Brooke planted ten acres on a six-hundred-foot mesa with optimal conditions for growing Rhône and Bordeaux varietals: maximum sun exposure, warm afternoons, cool evenings, and sandy loam soil.

At first the Carhartts sold most of their fruit to other winemakers. They converted a hay barn into a winery, and Brooke studied enology. In 1998, the first year of fruit production, they vinified two barrels for their own label bearing the Carhartt cattle brand. These early Merlots and Syrahs garnered favorable reviews and awards, so they continued to develop their own program and soon had enough wine to open a tasting room. Their current estate plantings include Sauvignon Blanc, Petite Sirah, and Grenache, alongside Sangiovese at neighboring 11 Oaks Vineyard. They also source Grenache Blanc, Pinot Noir, Cabernet Franc, Cabernet Sauvignon, and Petit Verdot from local sources.

Mike still spends part of every day in the vineyard, and Brooke and Chase manage the wine-making, but the Carhartts can also be found pouring in the tasting room. As the third generation of Carhartts out west, Chase continues the legacy of this farming and winemaking family.

CARR VINEYARDS & WINERY

Carr Winery, in the heart of downtown Santa Barbara, ranks among the most distinctive tasting rooms in the region. The red-and-white Quonset hut, which resembles a wine cave, originally served as a military barracks at Santa Barbara Airport during World War II. In 2006 winemaker Ryan Carr seized the opportunity to open a new winery and tasting room in the hut, which offered everything he sought: ample space for winemaking operations (4,500 square feet), a downtown location, and easy access via walking, cycling, or public transportation.

Ryan and his wife, Jessica, who serves as director of sales and marketing, immediately began transforming the hut into an efficient winemaking operation and attractive tasting room. They added eco-friendly insulation, tasting bar made by hand from eye-catching works of art such as a a wineglass and a forty-five-pound Outside, a tiny patio with redwood shaded tables beckons visitors to door opens to a cool, cavernous oak and stainless steel wine barrels,

fashioned a striking wraparound wine barrels, and decorated with whimsical robot figurine clutching longboard Ryan built in college. Adirondack chairs and umbrella-stop and enter the winery. The room, where guests can view the play tabletop shuffleboard, and listen to music while tasting Ryan's ultrapremium, limited-production wines. In the fall, visitors can watch Ryan and staff make and bottle wine in the same space.

Before launching his winemaking career, Ryan Carr studied plant science and majored in graphic design at the University of Arizona. After college, Carr headed to Santa Ynez, determined to build a career in winemaking. One of his first jobs was very hands-on—working in the fields for a local vineyard management company. In 1998 he was presented with the opportunity to make wine for Stolpman Vineyards at Central Coast Wine Services. A year later, he produced his first vintage—a total of ten cases—using grapes from a vineyard where he worked. The success of this initial effort inspired him to establish his own vineyard development company and winery.

Today Carr Vineyards supervises more than a hundred acres of vineyards throughout Santa Barbara County, including Paredon (Syrah and Grenache), Morehouse (Syrah), Vandale (Sangiovese), Turner (Pinot Noir, Syrah, and Pinot Gris), and the Yard (Pinot Noir). All Carr wines are made from Santa Barbara County grapes grown to Ryan Carr's exact specifications. He now specializes in Pinot Noir, Pinot Gris, and Cabernet Franc. Carr is a big fan of Grenache, but produces it in extremely limited quantities. He spends much of his time outdoors in the vineyards, but often stops by the winery to chat with visitors about his latest vintages.

CARR VINEYARDS & WINERY
414 N. Salsipuedes St.
Santa Barbara, CA 93103
805-965-7985
info@carrwinery.com
carrwinery.com

OWNER: Ryan Carr.

LOCATION: 6 blocks east of State St. at E. Gutierrez St.

APPELLATIONS: Happy Canyon of Santa Barbara, Santa Ynez Valley, Sta. Rita Hills.

HOURS: 11 A.M.–6 P.M. Sunday–Wednesday; 11 A.M.–8 P.M. Thursday–Saturday.

TASTINGS: $12–$15. Reservations requested for 8 or more guests. $15 tasting fee for groups over 20.

TOURS: None.

THE WINES: Cabernet Franc, Grenache, Pinot Gris, Pinot Noir, Sangiovese, Sauvignon Blanc, Syrah.

SPECIALTIES: Cabernet Franc, Pinot Gris, Pinot Noir.

WINEMAKER: Ryan Carr.

ANNUAL PRODUCTION: 4,500 cases.

OF SPECIAL NOTE: Wines by the glass, flights of wine, wine on tap, and tastings offered daily. Winemaker dinner, art shows, and other special events scheduled year-round. The winery has a second tasting room in Santa Ynez.

NEARBY ATTRACTIONS: East Beach and Cabrillo Bathhouse (city of Santa Barbara's main beach); Santa Barbara Zoo; Santa Barbara Waterfront District; historic Mission Santa Barbara; Santa Barbara Museum of Art.

COSTA DE ORO WINERY

COSTA DE ORO WINERY
1331 S. Nicholson Ave.
Santa Maria, CA 93454
805-922-1468
info@cdowinery.com
cdowinery.com

OWNERS: Burk and
Espinola families.

LOCATION: Just east of U.S.
101 at Stowell Rd. exit.

APPELLATION: Santa Maria
Valley.

HOURS: 11 A.M.–6 P.M. daily
plus Friday Night Wine
Down 5–8 P.M.

TASTINGS: $10 for 5 wines.

TOURS: None.

THE WINES: Cabernet
Sauvignon, Chardonnay,
Merlot, Pinot Grigio, Pinot
Noir, Sauvignon Blanc,
Syrah, Tempranillo.

SPECIALTIES: Estate
Chardonnay and
Pinot Noir.

WINEMAKER: Gary Burk.

ANNUAL PRODUCTION:
6,500 cases.

OF SPECIAL NOTE: Winery is
pet friendly. Deli case with
cheeses, meats, and crackers. Large gift shop with
wine-themed items, books,
and local arts and crafts.
On-site patio and picnic
area. Lounge area. Friday
Night Wine Down with live
music, wines by the glass,
and appetizers. Cabernet
Sauvignon, Sauvignon
Blanc, Syrah, Rosé, Merlot,
and Pinot Grigio available
only in tasting room.

NEARBY ATTRACTIONS: Pacific
Conservatory of the Per-
forming Arts (year-round
theater performances);
Santa Maria Museum
of Flight; Dunes Center
(exhibits on Guadalupe-
Nipomo Dunes Preserve).

Every Friday evening, local Santa Marians and visitors in the know head to the Costa de Oro Winery tasting room to celebrate the end of the workweek — and to launch the weekend in spirited style. They relax in the comfortable lounge, where they order appetizers and fine wines by the glass and bottle. They also listen to live music, ranging from rock to country and western, performed by various artists, including local Grammy Award winners and touring groups.

This unusual, beyond-the-bottle blend of music and wine reflects the dual passions of Costa de Oro winemaker/musician Gary Burk. His father, Ron Burk, and Bob Espinola founded Gold Coast Farms in 1978 in the heart of the Santa Maria Valley. Fruits and vegetables thrived there, except on a particular bluff — Fuglar's  Point. The farmers had a hunch that the bluff's well-drained, sandy loam soil, a poor match for vegetables, would make an ideal home for wine grapes. In 1989 the Burk and Espinola families planted thirty acres, twenty to Pinot Noir and ten to Chardonnay, with vine cuttings from the famed Sierra Madre Vineyard just a few miles away.

The hunch proved correct. Gold Coast Vineyard began producing fruit in the early 1990s. Gary Burk, a singer and guitarist, lived in Los Angeles at the time. He supplemented his performance income by selling Gold Coast Vineyard grapes to Au Bon Climat, Foxen, and other local wineries. In 1994 Jim Clendenen, owner/winemaker at Au Bon Climat, and Bob Lindquist, owner/winemaker at Qupé winery at Bien Nacido Vineyards, offered Gary an assistant winemaking position. Gary accepted and simultaneously started producing the first Costa de Oro wines — one barrel each of Pinot Noir and Chardonnay. Gary stayed at Au Bon Climat and Qupé until 2002, when he left to devote his full energies to Costa de Oro. His award-winning wines, praised for their European-style elegance and balance, focus almost exclusively on Pinot Noir and Chardonnay made from estate fruit and other Santa Maria Valley grapes. Gary also sources fruit from other Central Coast vineyards and crafts wines at a shared facility in Santa Maria. Costa de Oro also produces specially bottled vintages for Roy's restaurants and for the Halekulani, a luxury hotel in Hawaii.

The casual, Tuscan-style Costa de Oro tasting room, opened in 2006, includes a tasting bar, plus sofa seating and tables for lounging. Windows open up to expansive views across Santa Maria Valley. Gift items and gourmet foods line the wooden tables and display cases. The room provides a warm, comfortable setting for tasting throughout the day, but becomes an extra-special venue on Friday nights, when wine, music, and good times with friends fill the air.

D'ALFONSO-CURRAN WINES

Rural, two-lane Santa Rosa Road meanders sixteen miles through the pastoral Sta. Rita Hills appellation, following the Santa Ynez River on its westward run to the Pacific Ocean. It's one of the area's most scenic settings, home to centuries-old ranches, ancient Chumash encampments, farms, and deer and other wildlife. A twenty-minute drive west leads to historic Rancho La Viña. Once part of a vast Mexican land grant and family owned and operated since the 1860s, the 2,800-acre estate produces quality Pinot Noir grapes, walnuts, organic heirloom tomatoes, and other crops that thrive in the appellation's exceptional growing conditions. It also provides a home and custom winery facility for Bruno D'Alfonso and Kris Curran—names synonymous with world-class winemaking in

Santa Barbara County.

D'Alfonso worked from 1983 to 2005 as head wine-maker at Sanford Winery in Lompoc, where he crafted internationally acclaimed vin-tages. Curran met D'Alfonso in the early 1990s, worked at his side during crush, and quickly developed a passion for winemaking. In 2000 she was tapped as head winemaker at Sea Smoke Cellars, also in the Santa Rita Hills, where she created some of the nation's most sought-after Pinot Noirs. Eight years later, she was lured away to direct winemaking at Foley Estates Vineyard & Winery.

Today the husband-and-wife team focuses on their own collection of fine wines under four different labels. Wines bearing the D'Alfonso-Curran label showcase ultra-premium Pinot Noirs exclusively from the Santa Rita Hills and vineyard-designated Chardonnays from esteemed vineyards in Santa Barbara County. Di Bruno vintages celebrate Bruno D'Alfonso's heritage with red and white Italian varieties (Pinot Grigio, Sangiovese, Nebbiolo, and Merlot). The Curran label concentrates primarily on Spanish varietals such as Grenache, Grenache Gris, Grenache Blanc, and Tempranillo, as well as some Syrahs. BADGE wines feature blended Pinot Noirs and stainless steel Chardonnay.

A visit to the D'Alfonso-Curran winery facility at Rancho La Viña represents a rare opportunity to experience the hands-on, inner workings of a boutique, limited-production winery with expert guides: the winemakers themselves, accompanied by their beloved German shepherds. The pair, along with a small crew, perform all stages of wine production. They offer visits and winery tours by appointment only and tailor the schedule around winery operations that day and around visi-tors' particular interests. Guests can sample bottled wines as well as enjoy tank and barrel tastings. They are also known to regale guests with friendly banter as they explain—and demonstrate—their winemaking methods, widely acknowledged as some of the best in the business.

D'ALFONSO-CURRAN WINES
4457 Santa Rosa Rd., Ste. 5
Lompoc, CA 93436
805-736-9463
info@d-cwines.com
d-cwines.com

OWNERS: Kris Curran, Bruno D'Alfonso.

LOCATION: 10 miles west of U.S. 101 on Santa Rosa Rd.

APPELLATIONS: Sta. Rita Hills, Santa Ynez Valley.

HOURS: Strictly by appointment.

TASTINGS: Custom-tailored to visitors' wishes.

TOURS: By appointment.

THE WINES: Chardonnay, Grenache, Grenache Blanc, Grenache Rosé (dry), Mer-lot, Nebbiolo, Pinot Grigio, Pinot Noir, Sangiovese, Tempranillo.

SPECIALTIES: Vineyard-designated Pinot Noirs and Chardonnays, vineyard-designated Syrahs, Spanish varietals.

WINEMAKERS: Kris Curran, Bruno D'Alfonso.

ANNUAL PRODUCTION: 5,000 cases.

OF SPECIAL NOTE: Depend-ing on the winery opera-tions, it may be possible to arrange a tasting hosted by the winemakers. The winemakers also partner with guest chefs for events such as cooking demon-stration classes with wine pairings at various venues throughout the region. Current events are on winery website.

NEARBY ATTRACTIONS: Historic Mission La Purísima; Nojoqui Falls County Park (hiking trails, picnic areas near seasonal waterfall); Santa Ynez Val-ley Farms (organic farm stand and petting zoo).

DEMETRIA ESTATE WINERY

DEMETRIA ESTATE WINERY
6701 Foxen Canyon Rd.
Los Olivos, CA 93441
805-686-2345
Alexis@demetriaestate.com
demetriaestate.com

OWNERS: John, Sandra, and
Alexis Zahoudanis.

LOCATION: Main gate is
8 miles north of Los Olivos
on Foxen Canyon Rd.

APPELLATION: Santa Ynez
Valley.

HOURS: 11 A.M.–5 P.M.
by appointment.

TASTINGS: $20 for 5 or
6 wines.

TOURS: None.

THE WINES: Chardon-
nay, Cinsault, Counoise,
Grenache Blanc, Grenache
Noir, Marsanne, Mourvèdre,
Picpoul Blanc, Pinot Noir,
Riesling, Roussane, Syrah,
Tempranillo, Viognier.

SPECIALTIES: Cuvée Constan-
tine (red Rhône blend),
Cuvée Papou (white Rhône
blend), vineyard-designated
Pinot Noir.

WINEMAKER: Harry Waye.

ANNUAL PRODUCTION:
6,000–8,500 cases.

OF SPECIAL NOTE:
Tree-shaded outdoor
terrace with picnic tables
overlooking biodynamic
vineyards. Monthly evening
dinners and movies, June,
July, August, and Septem-
ber ($165 for two). Open
house for Santa Barbara
County Vintner's Festival
(April) and Harvest Festival (October). Pinot Noir
and Chardonnay available
only at tasting room.

NEARBY ATTRACTIONS:
Historic buildings in
Los Olivos and Ballard;
Clairmont Farm Lavender
Company; Quicksilver
Miniature Horse Ranch.

In Greek mythology, Demeter, the goddess of harvest, presides over all crops and the fertility of the Earth. Her name is a perfect symbol for Demetria Estate Winery, on 213 hilltop acres in the pastoral countryside north of Los Olivos. A visit to Demetria closely resembles a journey back in time to old-world landscapes reminiscent of ancient Greece. Guests drive along Foxen Canyon Road and pull up to the main gate, where they press a button to request permission to enter. From there, they follow a narrow, private road nearly two and a half miles to the winery, in an ocher Mediter-ranean building that is flanked by twenty-five-foot cypress trees and once served as a horse barn. The tasting room resembles a casual farm kitchen, with high ceilings, Spanish tile floors, replicas of Greek urns on high shelves, and wines poured at a rustic wooden table topped with granite. Olive, valley oak, and sycamore trees shade picnic tables on an expansive outdoor terrace, where guests are treated to scenic views of vineyards and live oaks on the hillside below.

This idyllic setting capti-vated John Zahoudanis when searching for vineyard property in 2005. He had grown up on a farm near Mount Olym-pus in Greece, where his family cultivated olives, citrus, and a small plot of grapes used to make wine for themselves. After World War II and the Greek civil war ravaged the farm, John's father moved the family to the United States. John studied economics at New York University, worked in commercial real estate, and married Sandra, a belle from South Carolina. They moved west and started a family. Later, John wanted to return to his farming and winemaking roots. He and Sandra purchased the estate and named it after their daughter, Demetria, and the aforementioned Greek goddess of harvest.

Today Demetria is still very much a family operation. John and Sandra's son, Alexis, has lived and worked on the estate full-time since 2009. He works closely with winemaker Harry Waye, who also oversees the vineyard—one of the first in Santa Barbara County to be farmed biody-namically—with forty-six acres planted to Rhône varietals, five white and five red. They also make Burgundian-style wines, sourcing organic Pinot Noir, Chardonnay, Pinot Blanc, and Pinot Gris grapes from trusted vineyards in cooler appellations, including La Encantada Vineyard in the Sta. Rita Hills and Sierra Madre and Presqu'isle vineyards in the Santa Maria Valley. The wines tend to reflect a natural, old-world character, with lower alcohol and high acidity that pair well with foods. Nearly all Demetria wines are made in small lots of five hundred cases or fewer, in much the same fashion as the Zahoudanis forefathers crafted wine on the family farm in Greece.

FESS PARKER WINERY & VINEYARD

Driving north along the pastoral Foxen Canyon Wine Trail feels like traveling back to California's early days. Rolling hills frame vast meadows, deer and other wildlife roam free, and pristine landscapes stretch as far as the eye can see. This peaceful environment enticed Fess Parker into buying a 714-acre ranch here back in 1988 The Texas-born actor, who played the television roles of Davy Crockett and Daniel Boone in the 1950s and 1960s, had moved his family to Santa Barbara in the early 1960s and begun construction of a blufftop home. When heavy rains caused it to collapse onto the beach, he revised his plans and headed inland.

There, he discovered the Foxen Canyon property, where he initially planned to run cattle, plant a few grapes to sell to other winery. Parker, an only child, business that he could pass asked his children to join him, experimental White Riesling spent three years as assistant helm in 1996. He then planted vintners, and establish a small dreamed of starting a family on to future generations. He and they planted a five-acre vineyard in 1989. Eli, his son, winemaker before taking the more vines and started a four-year project to build a cutting-edge winery and tasting room.

Today Eli Parker and his sister, Ashley Parker Snider, own and operate Fess Parker Winery and Vineyard. Ashley's husband, Tim Snider, is president. Most activities center around the 400-acre Foxen Canyon Road estate. The family grows most of their wine grapes in the on-site, 120-acre Rodney's Vineyard, named after Fess Parker's late son-in-law. They also source grapes from vineyards in the cooler Sta. Rita Hills and Santa Maria Valley appellations. Blair Fox assumed the role of head winemaker in 2005 In recent years, the winery has sharpened its focus to produce more small-lot, single-vineyard-designated wines made from high-quality Rhône and Burgundian varietals, which have won awards in national wine competitions.

Completed in 1994, the new winery and tasting room are loosely designed after an Australian sheep station, with a grand stone fireplace, stone floors, and a wraparound veranda with picnic tables. The spacious complex is set amid an acre of meticulously landscaped grounds that border the vineyard. The amphitheater-style lawn, rimmed by mature oaks, provides a serene setting for picnics, a summer-afternoon live music series, and other events. Indoors, visitors taste the latest vintages at a custom-crafted, polished concrete bar etched with images of coonskin caps. Photos of Fess Parker as Davy Crockett and Daniel Boone and other memorabilia related to the actor's television roles surround the spacious room—vivid testaments of the winery patriarch's remarkable legacy.

FESS PARKER WINERY & VINEYARD
6200 Foxen Canyon Rd.
Los Olivos, CA 93441
805-688-1545
800-841-1104
infowinery@fessparker.com
fessparkerwines.com

OWNER: Parker family.

LOCATION: 1.5 miles east of intersection of Foxen Canyon Rd. and Zaca Station Rd.

APPELLATION: Santa Ynez Valley.

HOURS: 10 A.M.–5 P.M. daily.

TASTINGS: $12 for 6 wines. $25 for 6 reserve wines, by appointment (includes tour).

TOURS: By appointment.

THE WINES: The Big Easy (red Rhône blend), Chardonnay, Pinot Noir, Riesling, Syrah, Viognier.

SPECIALTIES: Rhône and Burgundian varietals.

WINEMAKER: Blair Fox.

ANNUAL PRODUCTION: 65,000 cases.

OF SPECIAL NOTE: Gift shop with wine and home accessories, food and wine books, deli items and gourmet foods, and other merchandise. Large, grassy picnic area; bistro tables under veranda. Food-and-wine pairings in private VIP lounge ($40) by appointment. Parker Picnic Series with wine, food, and live music in summer months. American Tradition Reserve Pinot Noir, Syrah, and Chardonnay available only in tasting room. Winery also operates a hotel, spa, and restaurant in downtown Los Olivos.

NEARBY ATTRACTIONS: Historic buildings in Los Olivos and Ballard; Clairmont Farm Lavender Company; Quicksilver Miniature Horse Ranch.

FOLEY ESTATES VINEYARD & WINERY

FOLEY ESTATES VINEYARD & WINERY
6121 Hwy. 246
Lompoc, CA 93436
805-737-6222
tastingroom@foleywines.com
foleywines.com

OWNER: William Foley II.

LOCATION: 8 miles west of Buellton on Hwy. 246.

APPELLATION: Sta. Rita Hills.

HOURS: 11 A.M.–5 P.M. daily.

TASTINGS: $10 for 5 wines.

TOURS: None.

THE WINES: Chardonnay, Pinot Noir, Rosé, Syrah.

SPECIALTIES: Estate-grown Pinot Noir and Chardonnay from specific vineyard blocks.

WINEMAKER: Lorna Kreutz.

ANNUAL PRODUCTION: 40,000 cases.

OF SPECIAL NOTE: Wine-and-cheese pairing ($30) by appointment. Picnic areas on-site, some under patio awning. Well-stocked gift shop with clothing, books, gourmet food items, and wine-themed crafts. Certain block-designated Chardonnay and Pinot Noir vintages available only in tasting room.

NEARBY ATTRACTIONS: Historic Mission La Purísima; Old Town Lompoc Heritage Walk (1-mile scenic tour with 18 stops); Jalama Beach County Park (tidepooling, nature trails, camping, surfing).

Along Highway 246 between Lompoc and Buellton, a stunning scene leaps into view from the roadside: a series of fifty-nine vineyard blocks blanketing steep, south-facing hillsides and the gently sloping valley below. The setting is Rancho Santa Rosa (Lindsay's and Courtney's Vineyard East), home of Foley Estates Vineyard & Winery and part of the original 15,000-acre parcel granted by the Mexican government to former Presidio officer Francisco Cota's ten children in 1845.

Vintner Bill Foley, owner of Lincourt Vineyards in the Santa Ynez Valley since 1994, had successfully produced varietals suited for the region's warm climate. However, he hoped to establish a separate vineyard estate to focus on Pinot Noir, Chardonnay, Syrah, and other varietals that would thrive in the limestone  soils and cooling maritime effects of the Sta. Rita Hills appellation. In 1998, with topographical maps and data from extensive soil and climate research in hand, he scoured the region and discovered an ideal site—the 460-acre Rancho Santa Rosa, with elevations from 500 to 1,000 feet above sea level. He then launched an ambitious project patterned after practices common in Burgundy's Côtes d'Or. He divided 230 acres of planted vines into fifty-nine small blocks (average size less than four acres), each farmed, harvested, and vinified separately according to specifications unique to the particular soils, microclimate, and elevation. Foley refurbished former stables to house a 12,000-square-foot, state-of-the-art winery, and completed an adjacent 3,500-square-foot tasting room and event center in 2005.

The Foley Estates Burgundian-influenced wines, highly regarded by wine critics and sommeliers, are known for their diversity and rich character. Estate vineyard blocks now include Pinot Noir, Syrah, Cinsault, Pinot Gris, Grenache, Grüner Veltliner, Gewürztraminer, and Pinot Grigio. Winemaker Lorna Kreutz uses her extensive hands-on experience to transform the fruit into sought-after wines. She honed her skills at several Southern California wineries, including Longoria Wines, SummerWood Winery, and Niner Wine Estates. In 2011 she joined Foley Family Wines as assistant winemaker for Foley Estates and sister winery Lincourt.

The tasting room, in the spacious hospitality center, reflects the ranch's historic Spanish/Mexican roots in contemporary mission style, with light wood floors, a curved cherrywood tasting bar, and shelves displaying myriad items for purchase. Guests can sink into leather armchairs near a stone fireplace and enjoy the magnificent views of the surrounding oak-studded hills and multifaceted vineyard that defines the modern Rancho Santa Rosa.

FOLEY FOOD & WINE SOCIETY

At the southern end of New Zealand's North Island, home of the famed Marlborough wine region, lies Wharekauhau—a verdant, 5,000-acre sheep station overlooking Palliser Bay. In the 1840s, workers began to shear the flock and row bales of wool out to ships anchored in the bay. Early on, a brand was created to mark special sacks filled with premium-quality wool that merited higher prices. The image was of an oarlock, a U-shaped device used to hold oars in place. According to legend, the shape symbolizes good health, fortune, and spiritual contentment.

Present-day owners of Wharekauhau, also chose the oarlock as an apt symbol & Wine Society (FFWS). They three of their greatest passions: and exceptional travel experi- than a dozen wineries (together California, Oregon, Washington Bill Foley and his wife, Carol Johnson Foley, of their latest venture, the Foley Food launched it in 2012 to celebrate world-class wines, fine dining, ences. The Foleys own more called Foley Family Wines) in state, and New Zealand.

In 2013 the Foleys opened the ing room at the Bacara Resort & Spa, a Foley Food & Wine Society tast- Spanish Mediterranean–style complex above a rugged beach about 14 miles west of downtown Santa Barbara. It exclusively showcases all top-tier (reserve) wines from the various Foley wineries under the same roof. Napa Valley wineries include Kuleto and Merus, both lauded for their Cabernet Sauvignon vintages, and Foley Johnson, which focuses on wines from estate Bordeaux varietals and a small-lot series of signature bottlings crafted by winemakers in the Foley Family group. Sonoma County wineries include Chalk Hill, famed for its Russian River Valley Chardonnay, and legendary Sebastiani, established in 1904. Eos from Paso Robles receives raves for its Cabernets, Zinfandels, and Moscato dessert wines. In Santa Barbara County, Foley Estates is best known for its Santa Rita Hills Pinot Noir and Chardonnay wines, while Lincourt and Firestone Vineyard in the warmer Santa Ynez Valley produce Bordeaux, Burgundian, and Rhône vintages. Three Rivers Winery in Washington's Columbia Valley specializes in Bordeaux varietals.

An exceptionally broad range of Foley Family wines is available in the cozy and elegant, lodge-style tasting room with sandstone walls, leather sofas, and wrought-iron chandeliers. The Winery of the Month flight spotlights a particular Foley Family winery; the Dream Flight presents a selection of wines that reflect the diverse styles of different properties. Samples are poured at the wood-rimmed, copper bar or at wine barrel tables sprinkled throughout the room. Visitors are welcome to take a glass and walk along the bluff-top public access trails and enjoy the scenic oceanfront vistas, similar to those in New Zealand's Palliser Bay and Marlborough wine country.

FOLEY FOOD & WINE SOCIETY
8301 Hollister Ave.
Goleta, CA 93117
805-968-1614
tastingroom@foleyfood
andwinesociety.com
foleyfoodandwinesociety
.com

OWNERS: William Foley II and Carol Johnson Foley.

LOCATION: 14 miles west of Santa Barbara at Bacara Resort & Spa entrance.

APPELLATIONS Alexander Valley, Carneros, Chalk Hill, Coombsville, Napa Valley, Paso Robles, Russian River Valley, Rutherford, Santa Ynez Valley, Sonoma Valley, Sta. Rita Hills.

HOURS: 11 A.M.–7 P.M. daily.

TASTINGS: Winery of the Month: $10–$15 for 4–6 wines. Dream Flight (selection from different properties): $15 for 4–6 wines.

TOURS: None on-site.

THE WINES: Cabernet Franc, Cabernet Sauvignon, Chardonnay, Gewürztraminer, Malbec, Meritage, Merlot, Moscato, Petit Verdot, Petite Sirah, Pinot Blanc, Pinot Gris, Pinot Noir, proprietary blends, Riesling, Rosé, Sauvignon Blanc, Syrah, Zinfandel.

SPECIALTIES: Limited-production wines from Foley Family wineries in California, Oregon, Washington state, and New Zealand.

WINEMAKERS Various.

ANNUAL PRODUCTION: Unavailable.

OF SPECIAL NOTE: Opportunity to taste from entire Foley portfolio. Cheese plates available in tasting room. Private tours available to Foley Family wineries in Santa Barbara County.

NEARBY ATTRACTIONS: Refugio State Beach; El Capitan State Beach.

FOXEN

FOXEN
7600 Foxen Canyon Rd.
Santa Maria, CA 93454

FOXEN 7200
7200 Foxen Canyon Rd.
Santa Maria, CA 93454
805-937-4251
info@foxenvineyard.com
foxenvineyard.com

OWNERS: Bill Wathen,
Richard Doré.

LOCATION: 16 miles north
of the intersection of Hwy.
154 and Foxen Canyon Rd.

APPELLATIONS: Happy
Canyon of Santa Barbara,
Sta. Rita Hills, Santa Maria
Valley, Santa Ynez Valley.

HOURS: 11 A.M.–4 P.M. daily.

TASTINGS: $10 for 5 wines
at each tasting room.

TOURS: None.

THE WINES: Foxen:
Chardonnay, Chenin Blanc,
Grenache, Mourvèdre,
Pinot Noir, Syrah; foxen
7200: Cabernet Franc,
Cabernet Sauvignon,
Sangiovese, Sauvignon
Blanc.

SPECIALTIES: Single-vineyard,
small-production wines.
Foxen: Cuvée Jeanne Marie
(Rhône-style blend); foxen
7200: Volpino (Cabernet
Sauvignon/Merlot blend).

WINEMAKER: Bill Wathen.

ANNUAL PRODUCTION:
17,000 cases.

OF SPECIAL NOTE: Mission
(dessert wine) sold in
tasting rooms only.
Reservations required
for groups larger than 6.
Picnic tables on-site.

NEARBY ATTRACTION:
Historic 1875 San Ramon
Chapel (Benjamin Foxen
Memorial Chapel).

Friends for more than thirty years, Dick Doré and Bill Wathen forged the successful partnership behind Foxen and foxen 7200. Widely known as the Foxen Boys, the two began making wine together in 1985 with borrowed tools and Cabernet Sauvignon grapes from a Santa Maria vineyard. For twenty-four years, they crafted wine in a nearly two-hundred-year-old hay barn on Rancho Tinaquaic, originally an 8,874-acre Mexican land grant purchased by Doré's great-great-grandfather, Benjamin Foxen, in 1837. On weekends, they took turns running the tasting room in the family's weathered shack along the road. As they expanded their Bordeaux-based portfolio to include Rhône-, Burgundy-, and Cal-Italian-style wines, they earned a reputation for exquisite quality and irreverent fun.

The winemaking operation eventually outgrew the old barn, and in 2009 Doré and Wathen opened a new solar-powered tasting room and winery down the road from their historic tasting shack. Sided with earth-toned redwood, the buildings resemble western barns and have monitor-style roofs for added light and air flow. Mounted on the warehouse roof, 216 solar panels provide nearly all of the facility's energy needs. Dense plantings of native California species flourish in wide beds and a bio-swale that nearly surrounds the property.

A textured concrete path leads to the tasting room entryway. Beyond the french doors, open beams of knotty pine and double-hung oak-framed windows confirm the country theme. At two L-shaped tasting bars—clad with corrugated tin and topped with polished concrete counters—staff members pour Foxen Chardonnay, Pinot Noir, and Rhône-style wines. Out back, visitors can relax at café-style tables. Views of the canyon include the grass-covered hills of Rancho Tinaquaic, settled by Benjamin Foxen. An English sea captain, he branded his livestock with a nautical design that inspired the winery's distinctive anchor-shaped logo.

A few yards south of the patio, the estate's sustainably and dry-farmed Tinaquaic "Bajita" Vineyard, planted in 2008, supports six acres of Syrah, Cabernet Franc, and Petit Verdot. The winery's original estate Tinaquaic Vineyard was planted in 1989 and, along with the new "Bajita" blocks, is the only dry-farmed vineyard in Santa Barbara County. Its eleven acres, comprised of Chardonnay, Cabernet Franc, and Syrah, are on a hilltop opposite the original tasting room, now known as foxen 7200. Once a blacksmith shop serving nineteenth-century stagecoaches, the rustic shack features the Foxen Boys' Bordeaux-style and blended Cal-Italian wines. It boasts wall-sized sliding doors that open to the rolling hills of Rancho Tinaquaic, which is still owned by Doré's family.

GRASSINI FAMILY VINEYARDS

The Happy Canyon appellation occupies an extraordinary section of the Santa Ynez Valley in eastern Santa Barbara County. It sits 1,500 feet above sea level, where maritime fog typically arrives later in the evening and leaves by morning. Bordeaux grapes thrive on the steep slopes and gentle valleys. The long, hot days help ripen the sugars. But the cooling maritime influence, as much as fifty degrees lower than the daytime high, slows the ripening process, enabling grapes to develop rich character and balance.

Back when Larry and Sharon Grassini bought a hundred-acre ranch parcel in Happy Canyon in the 1980s, the area was virtually undiscovered as a wine region. After a neighbor planted a vineyard, the Grassinis asked a consulting  team to visit their own property to assess its grape-growing potential. The team marveled at the diversity of soils, slopes, and microclimates. In 2002 the Grassinis began to plant thirty-five acres of traditional Bordeaux varietals: Sauvignon Blanc, Cabernet Franc, Cabernet Sauvignon, Merlot, and Petit Verdot. The sustainably farmed vines are set in small, high-density blocks at various sites in the valley and on gently rolling hills, ridges, and steep slopes. The green-minded Grassinis also built a gravity-flow winery, using reclaimed antique fir from Washington's Columbia River. The winery and vineyard are solar powered, all water used in the winery is recycled, and irrigation water comes from the estate's lake, fed by two wells.

Grassini Family Vineyards today is famed for its flavor-packed grapes. The family-run company sells about half to select local winemakers and retains the remainder to make wines for its own label. Katie, the eldest of Larry and Sharon Grassini's four daughters, handles the daily operations. Wines are made in very limited quantities (most under five hundred cases). The Articondo, a Bordeaux blend, honors Larry Grassini's grandfather, who immigrated to Minneapolis from Pisa and introduced Larry to gardening during summer vacations. The Equipo ("team" in Spanish) wine reflects the Grassini family's commitment to sustainable communities; estate vineyard workers farm selected vines themselves each vintage, and proceeds go to year-end bonuses and emergency funds.

The Grassini Family Vineyards tasting room is in downtown Santa Barbara in the historic El Paseo, a shopping and dining complex built in the early 1920s to resemble a Spanish village. The tasting bar, tables, and shelves are all handcrafted from the same antique fir reclaimed from the Columbia River. Visitors can relax in leather recliners with a glass of wine and view scenic photos of Happy Canyon, in a constantly changing display on a seventy-inch flatscreen television.

GRASSINI FAMILY VINEYARDS
813 Anacapa St.,
El Paseo #6
Santa Barbara, CA 93101
805-897-3366
info@grassinifamily
vineyards.com
grassinifamilyvineyards
.com

OWNERS: Grassini family.

LOCATION: El Paseo complex next to Wine Cask Restaurant, 1 block east of State St., between Canon Perdido and De La Guerra Sts.

APPELLATION: Happy Canyon of Santa Barbara.

HOURS: Noon–6 P.M. daily. (Last tasting is at 5:30 P.M.)

TASTINGS: $10 for 4 or 5 wines. $30 for 5 to 7 reserve wines.

TOURS: None.

THE WINES: Cabernet Franc, Cabernet Sauvignon, Merlot, Petit Verdot, Sauvignon Blanc.

SPECIALTIES: Estate-grown Bordeaux varietals, Articondo Bordeaux blend.

WINEMAKER: Bradley Long.

ANNUAL PRODUCTION: 3,000 cases.

OF SPECIAL NOTE: Tasting room is pet friendly. Wines paired with locally made chocolate truffles daily ($10 in addition to tasting fee). Custom candles made from recycled wine bottles plus gifts and clothing available for purchase. Happy Canyon estate is open to public only on first weekend in October for annual Crush Cookout (barbecue and open house). Reserve and library wines available only in tasting room.

NEARBY ATTRACTIONS: Santa Barbara beaches, harbor, and waterfront; mission and other historic buildings; museums and zoo; Santa Barbara Art Foundry (bronze-casting tours).

HITCHING POST WINES

HITCHING POST WINES
The Hitching Post II
406 E. Hwy. 246
Buellton, CA 93427
805-688-0676
info@hitchingpostwines
.com
hpwines.com

OWNER: Frank Ostini.

LOCATION: .5 mile east of
U.S. 101.

APPELLATIONS: Santa Maria
Valley, Santa Ynez Valley,
Sta. Rita Hills.

HOURS: 4–6 P.M. Monday–
Friday; 3–5 P.M. Saturday
and Sunday (for wine
tasting).

TASTINGS: $7 for 4 wines.

TOURS: None.

THE WINES: Dry Rosé,
Merlot, Pinot Noir, Syrah.

SPECIALTY: Highliner Pinot
Noir.

WINEMAKERS: Gray Hartley,
Frank Ostini.

ANNUAL PRODUCTION:
18,000 cases.

OF SPECIAL NOTE: Tastings
are held in one of the most
popular restaurants in the
Santa Ynez Valley. Wines
are made by chef-owner to
complement menu.

NEARBY ATTRACTIONS:
OstrichLand USA (33-acre
ostrich farm); Elverhøj
Museum of History and
Art (exhibits on Danish
community in Solvang);
Santa Barbara Soaring
(glider rides); historic
Mission Santa Inés.

It's one thing to pair wines with food. But how many chefs crush, barrel, and bottle the wine served with the food they prepare? Chef-winemaker Frank Ostini set out to accomplish just that in 1979. His parents had operated the popular Hitching Post steak house in Casmalia, near Santa Maria, since 1952. They specialized in Santa Maria–style barbecue—grilling steaks and chops over an open fire of red oak. After Ostini returned from college in 1976, he worked in the Hitching Post kitchen. As a lark, he decided to create his own wines to complement the restaurant's meals. He asked a friend, Gray Hartley, to join him in the backyard project. Hartley agreed, and the duo made a Merlot in an old whis-key barrel. The next year, they produced a Cabernet, followed in 1981 by a Pinot Noir. Pleased with the results of their amateur Pinot Noir, a variety that had not yet emerged as a regional star, Ostini and Hartley went com-mercial in 1984 and soon gained critical acclaim for smooth vin-tages that matched extremely well with food.

In 1991 Hartley and Ostini produced enough wine to sell outside the restaurant. Because Hartley fished commercially in Alaska for more than twenty years, his seafaring days have influenced some of the winery's signature labels: the flagship Highliner Pinot Noir uses a term that refers to the best fisherman in the fleet. Hartley and Ostini give credit to the sources for their wines: prestigious vineyards throughout Santa Barbara County, including Julia's Vineyard, Bien Nacido, Fiddlestix, and Cargasacchi.

Ostini opened the Hitching Post II restaurant in Buellton in 1986. He retained the Santa Maria–style barbecue, but added eclectic ingredients such as quail and duck to the menu. Flights of Hitching Post wines are available for tasting in the wood-paneled lounge area. Bartenders pour the wine samples, and many visitors also order from the appetizer menu. The movie *Sideways* was filmed extensively at the restaurant in 2003, and photos of Ostini and the cast line the walls.

In 2008 Hartley and Ostini moved their winemaking operations from Santa Maria to Terravant Wine Company, a custom winemaking facility in Buellton. Although tastings of Hitching Post wines are offered at Terravant's new visitor center, wine aficionados continue to flock to the ever-popular Hitching Post II, where the chef-winemaker blends his culinary and vinous creations.

LORING/CARGASACCHI TASTING ROOM

Brian Loring has pursued an obsession with Pinot Noir since the early 1980s, when he worked at a wine shop stocked with great Pinot Noir from France. At the time Loring was not impressed with American versions of the variety. But one day he literally tripped over a case of Pinot Noir from Calera Wine Company, tried it, and liked it very much. He contacted winemaker Josh Jensen, who proved to Loring that first-rate Pinot Noir could be made in California. He vowed to open his mind and palate to domestic possibilities in the coming years.

For more than a decade, Loring pursued his Pinot Noir interests in his free time. One day, while attending a wine show, he tasted Cottonwood Canyon's 1990 Santa Maria Pinot Noir. The quality so impressed him that he 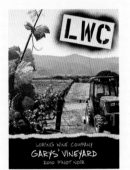 spent several years attending every Cottonwood Canyon event and conversing with winemaker Norm Beko. Beko invited Loring to learn firsthand during the 1997 crush. Loring then decided to launch the Loring Wine Company. His sister, Kimberly, began working with him in 2001. Since 2004, they have been co-owners and co-winemakers.

Today the Lorings are consid-ered some of the state's top Pinot Noir winemakers—their wines have made the *Wine Spectator* Top 100 list multiple years since 2004. Self-proclaimed nonfarmers, they are fanatical about sourcing grapes from trusted vineyards, including several in the nearby Sta. Rita Hills appellation. The Lorings give the growers free rein to farm their acres according to the same high standards in which they grow their own grapes. Brian and Kimberly decide when to pick the grapes, which often hang longer on the vine than most, resulting in bigger, bolder flavor, their signature style.

Brian Loring met Peter Cargasacchi in 2002 at a co-op winemaking facility in Buellton. Cargasacchi, whose Italian family has farmed in the Central Coast since the early 1900s, planted the twelve-acre Cargasacchi Vineyard in the Sta. Rita Hills in 1998 and the nearby Jalama and Levante vineyards in subsequent years. He has sold grapes to the Lorings since 2003. Most fruit is contracted to top-tier winemakers like the Lorings. But Cargasacchi retains a small portion to produce wines under his Cargasacchi and Point Concepción labels.

A wrought-iron rooster and hen atop a rustic gate welcome travelers to the new Loring/Cargasac-chi tasting room, opened in 2013 in a pre–World War II farmhouse in Buellton between the Hitch-ing Post II restaurant (famed from the film *Sideways*) and an ostrich ranch. The ten-acre grounds include bluff-top picnic areas overlooking the wildlife roaming the meadows along the Santa Ynez River—a scenic setting for savoring the results of the Loring and Cargasacchi winemaking efforts.

LORING/CARGASACCHI TASTING ROOM
420 E. Hwy. 246
Buellton, CA 93427
805-691-1300
April@loringwinecompany
.com
loringwinecompany.com
cargasacchi.com

OWNERS: Brian Loring and Kimberly Loring; Peter Cargasacchi.

LOCATION: .5 mile east of U.S. 101.

APPELLATIONS: Loring: Russian River Valley, Santa Lucia Highlands, Sonoma Coast, Sta. Rita Hills. Cargasacchi: Santa Barbara County, Santa Maria Valley, Sta. Rita Hills.

HOURS: 10 A.M.–5 P.M. Thursday–Monday.

TASTINGS: $10 for 5 wines.

TOURS: None.

THE WINES: Loring: Chardonnay, Pinot Noir. Cargasacchi: Chardonnay, Merlot, Pinot Grigio, Pinot Noir.

SPECIALTIES: Vineyard-designated Pinot Noir (both).

WINEMAKERS: Brian Loring and Kimberly Loring; Peter Cargasacchi.

ANNUAL PRODUCTION: Loring: 7,000 cases. Cargasacchi: 1,500 cases.

OF SPECIAL NOTE: Scenic picnic areas overlooking Santa Ynez River.

NEARBY ATTRACTIONS: OstrichLand USA (33-acre ostrich ranch); Elverhøj Museum of History and Art (exhibits on Danish community in Solvang); Santa Barbara Soaring (glider rides); historic Mission Santa Inés; Wildling Art Museum (art of the American wilderness).

PALI WINE CO.

PALI WINE CO.
116 E. Yanonali St.
Santa Barbara, CA 93101
805-560-7254
stacey@paliwineco.com
paliwineco.com

LOMPOC TASTING ROOM:
1501 E. Chestnut Ct.

WINERY:
1036 W. Aviation Dr.
Lompoc, CA 93436
805-735-2354

OWNER: Tim Perr,
managing partner.

LOCATION: Santa Barbara:
Yanonali St. at Gray Ave.
Lompoc: .3 mile from Hwy.
246 via 7th St. Winery:
1 mile west of Hwy. 1.

APPELLATIONS: Sta. Rita
Hills, Santa Barbara County,
Russian River Valley,
Sonoma Coast, Willamette
Valley (Oregon).

HOURS: Santa Barbara:
11 A.M.–6 P.M. daily.
Lompoc: 11 A.M.–5 P.M.
Thursday–Sunday,
11 A.M.–6 P.M. Saturday.

TASTINGS: $10 for 5 wines.
Tastings at winery by
appointment.

TOURS: None.

THE WINES: Pali: Chardon-
nay, Pinot Noir. Tower 15:
Rhône and Bordeaux vari-
etals, The Jetty (Grenache,
Syrah, Mourvèdre, Petite
Sirah), The Swell (Cabernet
Sauvignon, Cabernet Franc,
Petit Verdot, Malbec, and
Merlot).

SPECIALTIES: Pali: Pinot Noir
and Chardonnay cuvées.
Tower 15: Rhône and Bur-
gundian varietal cuvées.

WINEMAKERS: Kenneth
Juhasz and Aaron Walker.

ANNUAL PRODUCTION:
40,000 cases.

OF SPECIAL NOTE: Santa
Barbara: Cheese plates and
chocolate available on-site.
Happy hour on Thursdays
and live music on Sundays.

Pacific Palisades (called "Pali" by locals) is a classic beach community on the Pacific Coast Highway between Malibu and Santa Monica. Residents often gather at the white-sand beach that borders the town to surf, play, and celebrate life events. Among these beach-going residents is entrepreneur Tim Perr, who started a highly successful actuarial consulting business here. He is also a savvy wine collector who has long enjoyed traveling to wine regions in California, Oregon, and abroad. Perr wanted to start a second business, and wines seemed a perfect fit. In 2005 he and his business partner, Scott Knight, founded Pali Wine Co., to showcase the *terroir* of top Pinot Noir–producing regions — Russian River Valley, Sonoma Coast, Santa Barbara County, Sta. Rita Hills, and Willamette

Valley — under a single label.

That same year, Pali pro- duced its first vintage of 1,500 cases of small-lot, single-vineyard Pinot Noir. In 2007 the company built a state-of-the-art winery facility in Lompoc near the Sta. Rita Hills appellation in northern Santa Barbara County, where consulting winemaker Kenneth Juhasz and on-site winemaker Aaron Walker oversee all facets of production, from crush to bottling. Pali continues to produce a top-tier line of critically acclaimed single-vineyard Pinot Noir and Chardonnay wines in small lots (maximum two hundred cases). Early on, Perr, who admittedly detests "wine snobbery," also wanted to offer accessible, value-laden wines to a broad range of customers. In 2007 Pali created its first cuvées, appellation-specific vineyard blends named for Pacific Palisades neighborhoods: Charm Acres Chardonnay, Sonoma Coast; Alphabets Pinot Noir, Willamette Valley; Riviera Pinot Noir, Sonoma Coast; Huntington Pinot Noir, Santa Barbara County; Summit Pinot Noir, Sta. Rita Hills; and Bluffs Pinot Noir, Russian River Valley. In 2012 Pali Wine Co. launched a new label, Tower 15, named for an iconic lifeguard tower in Pacific Palisades. Tower 15 wines focus exclusively on the diverse Rhône and Bordeaux varietals grown in Paso Robles.

Visitors can taste Pali and Tower 15 wines at two sites. In 2013 Pali Wine Co. carved out a tast- ing room space in its barrel room in the Lompoc Wine Ghetto, a cluster of circa twenty wineries in an industrial park. The decor matches the *garagiste* setting, with a bar made of recycled barn wood and corrugated metal. The main downtown Santa Barbara tasting room, opened in 2012, is in the hip Funk Zone near the waterfront. Guests can taste wines at the redwood-mahogany bar and fill glasses and growlers (containers) with fresh barrel wines from kegs. Two blocks away is Santa Bar- bara's famed East Beach, where visitors and locals alike revel in activities similar to those in Pacific Palisades, just a little more than an hour's drive to the south.

SANFORD WINERY & VINEYARDS

In spring and early summer, colorful wildflowers blanket the slopes and meadows of the Santa Rita Hills, which flank the Santa Ynez River on its westward trek to the Pacific Ocean about twenty miles away. Sanford Winery & Vineyards rests in a valley in the heart of this captivating landscape, a veritable Shangri-la surrounded by vineyards and pristine vistas. Friends Richard Sanford and Michael Benedict discovered this hidden spot in 1970 and planted the first Pinot Noir vineyard in Santa Barbara County in 1971. Chardonnay and Pinot Noir grapes from their Sanford & Benedict Vineyard eventually helped launch Sanford Winery and the entire region into international wine-scene stardom.

Thanks in large part to Sanford Winery's stellar reputation for outstanding Burgundian estate wines, the Sta. Rita Hills became an official AVA in 2001. Though Mr. Sanford and Mr. Benedict no longer have ties to the vineyard, Sanford Winery & Vineyards continues to cultivate the much-lauded grapes in diverse blocks at the 500-acre Sanford & Benedict ranch (135 acres under vine) and in the adjacent 438-acre La Rinconada Vineyard (130 acres under vine). Winemaker Steve Fennell transforms the fruit into fine wines at the on-site winery at the La Rinconada property, an eco-friendly facility built in 2006 with hand-formed adobe bricks and timbers from a century-old barn in Washington state. Fennell crafts six Pinot Noir and three Chardonnay wines each vintage with fruit sourced exclusively from the two estate vineyards and plans to introduce more small-lot bottlings. The winery also produces a small number of other varieties, such as Sauvignon Blanc, from local vineyards.

A visit to Sanford Winery & Vineyards is a complete, all-in-one winery experience. The two-story tasting room building adjoins the winery and is built with reclaimed barnwood, native California stone, and more than 15,000 handmade adobe bricks. Guests can join vineyard tours, sample wines, or have a seated tasting in the stunning Spanish-Mediterranean tasting room, and enjoy 360-degree views of the winery and vineyards on shaded front and back terraces.

In 2013 Sanford Winery opened a second tasting room in downtown Santa Barbara in historic La Arcada, a collection of restaurants, galleries, and shops in a charming plaza with artworks dating back to its 1926 origin. The atmosphere is urban chic, but connects visitors to the rural Santa Rita Hills location via a slideshow on an eighty-inch high-definition flatscreen television, reclaimed barnwood columns from the Sanford & Benedict Vineyard, and oak beams from the winery property. Staff at both tasting rooms pour a full range of Sanford wines, from bottles with custom-designed labels depicting wildflowers that blossom, in season, around the iconic vineyards.

SANFORD WINERY & VINEYARDS
5010 Santa Rosa Rd.
Lompoc, CA 93436
800-426-9463
info@sanfordwinery.com
sanfordwinery.com

DOWNTOWN SANTA BARBARA:
1114 State St., Ste. 26
Santa Barbara, CA 93101
805-770-7873
SBtastingroom@sanford
winery.com

OWNERS: Terlato Family.

LOCATION: Santa Rita Hills: 10 miles west of U.S. 101 and Buellton. Downtown Santa Barbara: In La Arcada Plaza.

APPELLATION: Sta. Rita Hills.

HOURS: Santa Rita Hills: 11 A.M.–4 P.M. daily, until 5 P.M. Friday and Saturday seasonally. Downtown Santa Barbara: noon–6 P.M. daily, until 7 P.M. Friday and Saturday seasonally.

TASTINGS: $15 for 6 wines. $20 for 5 or 6 reserve wines.

TOURS: Tour and tasting daily at 11:30 A.M. ($30) by reservation.

THE WINES: Chardonnay, Pinot Noir, Sauvignon Blanc, Vin Gris.

SPECIALTIES: Estate Chardonnay and Pinot Noir.

WINEMAKER: Steve Fennell.

ANNUAL PRODUCTION: 30,000 cases.

OF SPECIAL NOTE: Vertical tastings and other special experiences by appointment ($80–$100). Block-designated Chardonnay and Pinot Noir. Picnic tables on lawn and covered patio at Santa Rita Hills location. Wine-themed gifts, clothing, and locally made food items available for purchase at both tasting rooms.

SILVER WINES

SILVER WINES
724 Reddick St.
Santa Barbara, CA 93103
805-963-3052
silverwines@aol.com
silverwines.com

OWNERS: Benjamin
and Thi Silver.

LOCATION: Between N.
Nopal and N. Quarantina
Sts., 1.5 blocks west of N.
Milpas St.

APPELLATIONS: Various in
Santa Barbara County.

HOURS: 11 A.M.–5 P.M.
Friday–Sunday, and by
appointment.

TASTINGS: $8 for 5 wines.

TOURS: None.

THE WINES: Cabernet Franc,
Cabernet Sauvignon,
Chardonnay, Grenache
Blanc, Nebbiolo, Pinot Noir,
Sangiovese, Syrah, Viognier.

SPECIALTIES: I Tre Figli
(Sangiovese, Cabernet
Sauvignon, Cabernet
Franc blend), Saviezza
(Sangiovese blend).

WINEMAKER:
Benjamin Silver.

ANNUAL PRODUCTION:
1,800 cases.

OF SPECIAL NOTE: Winemaker often present in
tasting room. Small-
production wines, including
Sweet "T" Viognier dessert
wines, available only in
tasting room. Annual events
include the Santa Barbara
County Vintner's Festival
(April) and Harvest Festival
(October). Tasting room is
on the Santa Barbara Urban
Wine Trail.

NEARBY ATTRACTIONS: Santa
Barbara beaches, harbor,
and waterfront; mission
and other historic build-
ings; museums and zoo;
Santa Barbara Art Foundry
(guided bronze-casting
tours).

Santa Barbara's Urban Wine Trail includes more than twenty wineries in the downtown area. Most cluster in the tourist hub near the waterfront. A handful, however, lie off the beaten track in the vibrant Lower Eastside neighborhood, an eclectic mix of multicultural restaurants, shops, residences, and small businesses. Silver Wines occupies a modest two-story building on a two-block street in the heart of this district, tucked between two early 1900s residences.

This down-home neighborhood provides an ideal environment for winemaker Benjamin Silver to craft fine wines and explore new blends and techniques. Silver was born to experiment — it's in his genes. He grew up in Amherst, where his father taught organic chemistry at Amherst College. In college, he planned to become a veterinarian. But a seven-month study abroad program in Siena, Italy, introduced him to excellent food and wines, and his experi- ence inspired him to learn to make his own wines and sell them. He returned to the University of Massachusetts to complete double bachelor degrees in animal science and Italian, and in the summer of 1993, he worked at Chicama Vineyards on Martha's Vineyard. After graduating the next summer, Silver packed up his car and drove cross-country to Santa Barbara

County to work as a harvest lab technician with established winemaker Daniel Gehrs at Zaca Mesa Winery. Following the harvest, the winery offered him a full-time lab supervisor position. Gehrs took Silver under his wing as an apprentice winemaker.

After Gehrs departed Zaca Mesa in 1997, Silver took over Zaca Mesa's winemaking helm and also began to experiment with small quantities of Zinfandel, Sauvignon Blanc, Cabernet Franc, and Nebbiolo. The results inspired Silver to leave Zaca Mesa in 2000 to develop his own label. He sources grapes only from trusted Santa Barbara County vineyards and makes "bottled snapshots" of the individual vineyards in that year, with a light alcohol content that doesn't mask fruit character. Silver specializes in two super Tuscan (aka Cal-Ital) red blend lines: Saviezza (Italian for "wisdom" or "knowledge"), a traditional Sangiovese-based blend aged in large-format barrels, and I Tre Figli (Italian for "the three sons"), a Sangiovese, Cabernet Sauvignon, and Cabernet Franc blend aged in large-format barrels. Visitors taste Benjamin Silver's vintages at a handcrafted wooden tasting bar in a sparsely furnished room where the wines themselves take center stage.

ZACA MESA WINERY & VINEYARDS

The Foxen Canyon Wine Trail snakes its way for twenty miles through some of California's most scenic countryside. At its highest point is a wild region, where deer, mountain lions, and even black bears still roam the hills. The native Chumash revered the site, calling it *zaca*, or "restful place."

In 1972 a group including real estate investor John Cushman purchased the 1,750-acre property, which was originally part of the 1830s Rancho La Zaca Mexican land grant. In 1973 they started the Zaca Mesa vineyard on soil that was once covered in prehistoric ocean dunes. Initial plantings included Cabernet Sauvignon, Chardonnay, Merlot, Zinfandel, Pinot Noir, and Riesling. The early fruit and vintages showed great promise, and in 1978 Zaca Mesa built a winery, which was expanded three years later into one of the region's first tasting rooms. In 1978 Zaca Mesa planted the first Syrah in Santa Barbara County, in a vineyard block that continues to provide low-yield grapes with intense flavor for the winery's coveted Black Bear Block Syrah. Many now-famous winemakers spent their early years at Zaca Mesa and later founded their own labels. Few other vineyards existed in the region in the early 1970s.

Zaca Mesa experimented with grape varieties for twenty years to determine which grew best in their microclimates and soils. This grape-growing experience determined Zaca Mesa's path from the 1990s onward: Rhône varieties prosper here, warmed by the sun early in the day and cooled by ocean breezes flowing through Los Alamos Valley to the vineyard from thirty miles away. The winery shifted its focus to Syrah and Rhône blends with great success. *Wine Spectator* placed the 1993 Zaca Mesa Syrah sixth on its Top 100 Wines list in 1995 and in 2010 ranked the 2006 Syrah at twenty-ninth.

Zaca Mesa now nurtures 200 acres of vineyards, follows sustainable growing practices, and takes a minimalist approach to winemaking. The visitor center, a lofty cedar structure designed to fit into the surroundings, looks much the same as it did nearly thirty years ago: cedar floors, soaring two-story ceilings, and gifts, cheeses, olives, and crackers displayed atop oak barrels. A U-shaped tasting bar with an aged zinc top and wood planks evokes the same rustic character as the original room. Outdoors, visitors are encouraged to sit in the grassy, oak-shaded courtyard, where they can play chess with knee-high pieces, picnic, and relax in ancient Chumash territory.

ZACA MESA WINERY & VINEYARDS
6905 Foxen Canyon Rd.
Los Olivos, CA 93441
805-688-9339
800-350-7972
info@zacamesa.com
zacamesa.com

OWNERS: John and Lou Cushman.

LOCATION: 9.4 miles north of Hwy. 154.

APPELLATION: Santa Ynez Valley.

HOURS: 10 A.M.–4 P.M. daily.

TASTINGS: $10 for 6 wines.

TOURS: By appointment.

THE WINES: Chardonnay, Grenache, Mourvèdre, Roussanne, Syrah, Viognier, Z Blanc (Roussanne, Grenache Blanc, Viognier blend), Z Cuvée (Grenache, Mourvèdre, Syrah, Cinsault blend, depending on vintage), Z Gris (rosé), Z Three (Syrah, Grenache, Mourvèdre blend).

SPECIALTIES: Chapel G Syrah, Grenache Blanc, Mesa Reserve Syrah, Black Bear Block Syrah.

WINEMAKER: Eric Mohseni.

ANNUAL PRODUCTION: 35,000 cases.

OF SPECIAL NOTE: Grassy courtyard with picnic tables and life-size chessboard. Hiking trail rises to spectacular views of Foxen Canyon.

NEARBY ATTRACTION: Historic 1875 San Ramon Chapel (Benjamin Foxen Memorial Chapel).

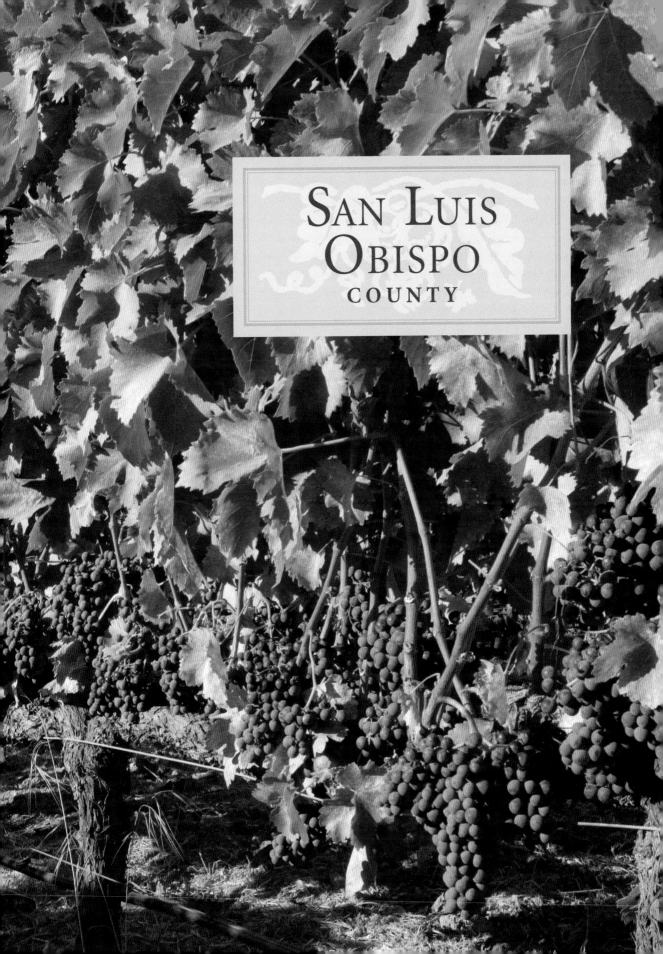

SAN LUIS OBISPO
COUNTY

San Luis Obispo County is divided into two distinct growing regions by the rugged Santa Lucia Range. Rising parallel to the coastline, the range separates the south, with its volcanic soils and mild, maritime climate, from the north, a region of fossil-studded soils and fifty-degree temperature swings. U.S. 101, extending north-south through the county, crosses the range at Cuesta Grade, where coastal plains meet the higher elevation oak woodlands. Along the coast, Highway 1 winds past the towns of Cambria, Morro Bay, and Pismo Beach. North at San Simeon, the magnificent Hearst Castle overlooks the Pacific Ocean.

In 1922 San Luis Obispo County's nascent wine industry garnered international attention when Polish pianist Ignace Paderewski planted Zinfandel vines near Paso Robles. When the 1960s brought success with Pinot Noir in vineyards on the west side of Paso Robles, wine grapes began to replace cattle ranches and hot springs as the county's dominant features. The 1973 planting of Paragon Vineyard established Edna Valley, near the city of San Luis Obispo, as a prime grape-growing area. Since the early 1980s, vinicultural growth has exploded, especially in the region north of Cuesta Grade, which is home to 75 percent of San Luis Obispo County's two-hundred-plus wineries. In 2013 *Wine Enthusiast* magazine named Paso Robles the Wine Country Region of the Year.

In response to industry expansion, local viticulturists formed the Central Coast Vineyard Team to promote sustainable farming. The group developed a program called Sustainability in Practice (SIP), featuring a rigorous set of standards in areas ranging from environmental stewardship to labor relations. Wineries and vineyards meeting these standards earn SIP certification, which verifies their efforts to protect workers, the environment, and business stability. To date, fifty California wineries, 31,000 vineyard acres, and 900,000 cases of wine have been SIP certified.

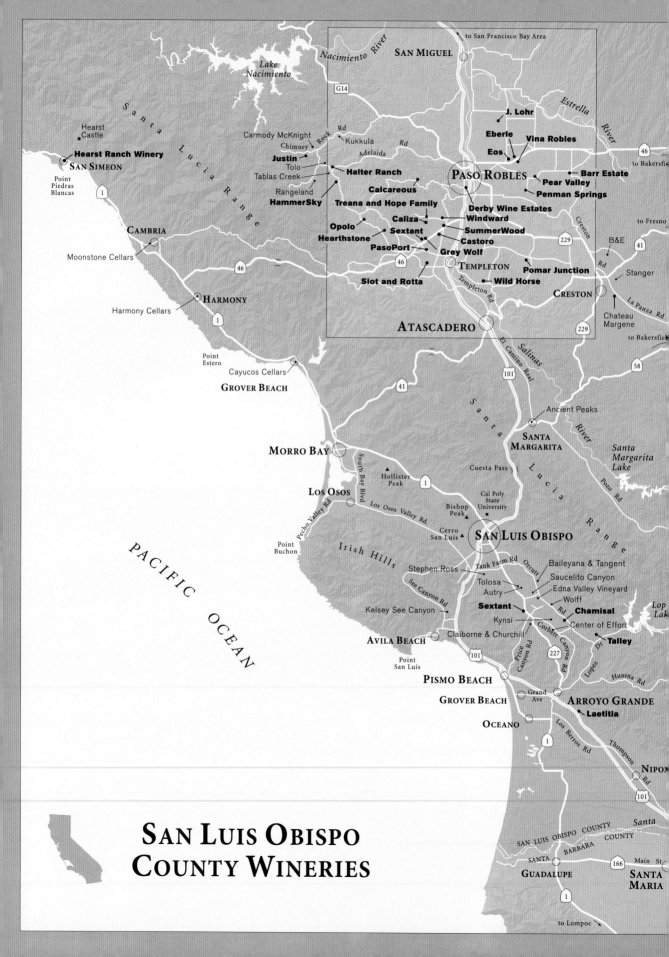

to San Francisco Bay Area

Nacimiento River

SAN MIGUEL

Lake Nacimiento

Santa Lucia Range

Hearst Castle

G14

J. Lohr

Eberle

Vina Robles

Carmody McKnight

Kukkula

Eos

Chimney

Rd

Rock

Adelaida

Rd

Estrella River

Justin

Tolo

Tablas Creek

Halter Ranch

PASO ROBLES

Barr Estate

Pear Valley

Penman Springs

Hearst Ranch Winery

SAN SIMEON

Point Piedras Blancas

Rangeland

Calcareous

Derby Wine Estates

HammerSky

Treana and Hope Family

Windward

SummerWood

46

to Bakersfie

46

Opolo

Caliza

Sextant

Castoro

Creston

229

B&E

41

to Fresno

MOONSTONE CELLARS

Hearthstone

PasoPort

Grey Wolf

Rd

Stanger

CAMBRIA

TEMPLETON

Pomar Junction

Siot and Rotta

Wild Horse

CRESTON

Chateau Margene

to Bakersfie

HARMONY

Templeton Rd

229

La Panza Rd

Harmony Cellars

1

ATASCADERO

El Camino Real

Salinas

58

Point Estero

101

GROVER BEACH

Cayucos Cellars

41

Santa Lucia Range

Ancient Peaks

Santa Margarita River

Santa Margarita Lake

SANTA MARGARITA

Pozo Rd

MORRO BAY

South Bay Blvd

Hollister Peak

Cuesta Pass

1

Cal Poly State University

LOS OSOS

Los Osos Valley Rd

Bishop Peak

Pecho Valley Rd

Cerro San Luis

SAN LUIS OBISPO

PACIFIC OCEAN

Point Buchon

Irish Hills

Baileyana & Tangent

Stephen Ross

Tank Farm Rd

Orcutt

Saucelito Canyon

Edna Valley Vineyard

See Canyon Rd

Tolosa

Autry

Wolff

Kelsey See Canyon

Sextant

Chamisal

Kynsi

Center of Effort

Lop Lak

Claiborne & Churchill

Corbett Canyon Rd

Talley

AVILA BEACH

227

Dr

Point San Luis

101

Price Canyon Rd

Lopez Dr

Huasna Rd

PISMO BEACH

GROVER BEACH

Grand Ave

ARROYO GRANDE

Laetitia

OCEANO

Los Berros Rd

Thompson Rd

1

NIPOM

101

Santa

SAN LUIS OBISPO COUNTY

SANTA BARBARA COUNTY

SANTA

GUADALUPE

166

Main St

SANTA MARIA

1

to Lompoc

SAN LUIS OBISPO COUNTY WINERIES

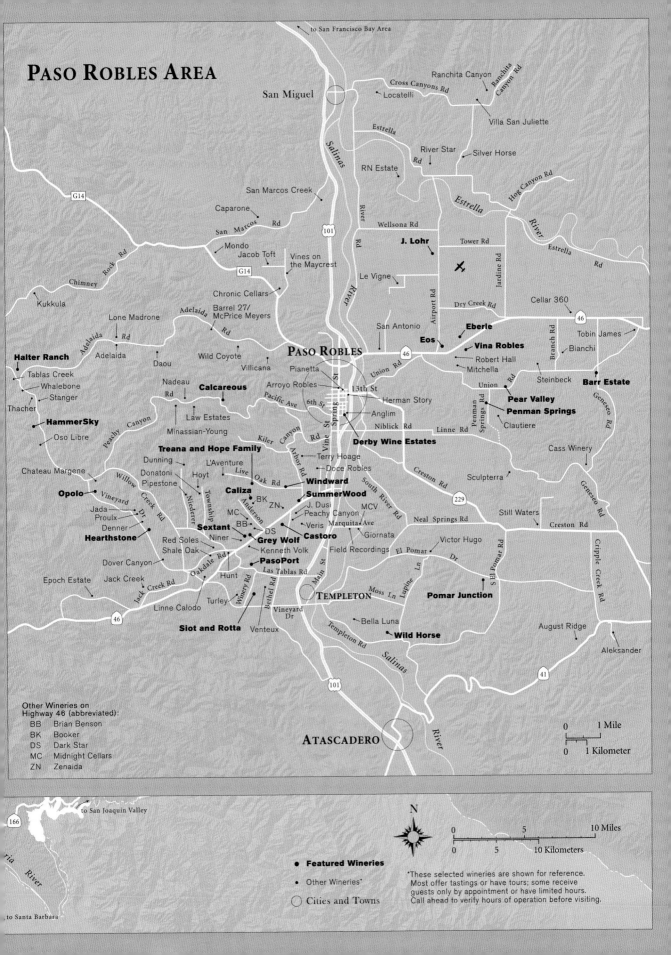

PASO ROBLES AREA

to San Francisco Bay Area

San Miguel

Ranchita Canyon
Cross Canyons Rd
Locatelli
Ranchita Canyon Rd
Villa San Juliette

Estrella

River Star
Rd
Silver Horse

RN Estate

Hog Canyon Rd

San Marcos Creek

G14

Caparone

San Marcos Rd

101

River Rd

Wellsona Rd

J. Lohr
Tower Rd

Estrella River
Estrella Rd

Mondo
Jacob Toft
Vines on the Maycrest

G14

Le Vigne

Airport Rd

Jardine Rd

Cellar 360

46

Chronic Cellars

Barrel 27/
McPrice Meyers

Adelaida Rd

San Antonio

Dry Creek Rd

Tobin James

Kukkula

Chimney Rock Rd

Lone Madrone

Adelaida Rd

Eberle

Eos

Vina Robles

Robert Hall
Mitchella

Branch Rd

Bianchi

Steinbeck

Barr Estate

PASO ROBLES

Pianetta

Union Rd

Halter Ranch
Tablas Creek
Whalebone
Stanger
Thacher
HammerSky
Oso Libre

Adelaida
Daou
Nadeau Rd
Wild Coyote
Villicana

Calcareous

Law Estates
Minassian-Young

Arroyo Robles
Pacific Ave
6th St
13th St

Vine St

Herman Story
Anglim
Niblick Rd

Union

Pear Valley
Penman Springs

Clautiere

Penman Springs Rd

Cass Winery

Geneseo Rd

Peachy Canyon

Terry Hoage
Doce Robles

Derby Wine Estates

Linne Rd

Treana and Hope Family
Dunning
Donatoni
Pipestone
Hoyt

L'Aventure

Live Oak Rd

Arbor Rd

Windward

SummerWood

Caliza

BK ZN

J. Dusi
Peachy Canyon
Veris

MCV

Marquita Ave

Field Recordings

Giornata

Creston Rd

Sculpterra

229

Chateau Margene
Opolo
Jada
Proulx
Denner
Hearthstone

Vineyard Dr

Willow Creek Rd

Township Rd

Niederer

MC

BB

DS

Sextant
Niner

Castoro

Grey Wolf

Anderson Rd

South River Rd

Neal Springs Rd

Still Waters

Creston Rd

Geneseo Rd

Cripple Creek Rd

Red Soles
Shale Oak
Kenneth Volk

PasoPort

Dover Canyon
Jack Creek

Oakdale Rd

Hunt

Epoch Estate

46

Linne Calodo

Jack Creek Rd

Turley

Winery Rd

Bethel Rd

Las Tablas Rd

Main St

Vineyard Dr

TEMPLETON

Victor Hugo

El Pomar Dr

Lupine Ln

S El Pomar Rd

Pomar Junction

Moss Ln

Bella Luna

Siot and Rotta

Venteux

Wild Horse

Templeton Rd

Salinas

August Ridge

Aleksander

101

ATASCADERO

River

41

Other Wineries on
Highway 46 (abbreviated):
BB   Brian Benson
BK   Booker
DS   Dark Star
MC   Midnight Cellars
ZN   Zenaida

0   1 Mile

0   1 Kilometer

to San Joaquin Valley

166

N

0   5   10 Miles

0   5   10 Kilometers

Nacimiento River

to Santa Barbara

● Featured Wineries

○ Other Wineries*

◯ Cities and Towns

*These selected wineries are shown for reference.
Most offer tastings or have tours; some receive
guests only by appointment or have limited hours.
Call ahead to verify hours of operation before visiting.

Barr Estate Winery

A young olive orchard and generous acre of Petite Sirah frame the country-lane entry at Barr Estate Winery. Bordering the vineyard, shrub roses bloom in a riot of color. Greg and Tealy Barr, who bought the eighty-five-acre property in 2007, run a family operation specializing in handcrafted artisan wines that are fruit forward and full-bodied with a lasting finish. Tealy tends the tasting room, daughter Mathilde oversees wine sales in Northern California, and son Geoff manages the vineyard. Greg handles the winemaking with help from noted consultant Signe Zoller, the region's first female winemaker, who came to Paso Robles in 1994.

Greg, a mechanical engineer, retired in 2004 after traveling the world with a company that manufactures gas turbines. The family lived in Iran, Greece, England, and Belgium, where Tealy and Greg enjoyed European wines. Upon returning to California in 1990, the couple developed a passion for California vintages that triggered a desire to make wine. The Barrs especially liked the wines of Paso Robles, where they found a friendly community, as well as ideal vineyard property located along a popular wine trail. Greg enrolled in and completed the Winemaking Certificate Program at U.C. Davis to learn how to grow and make wine, and often turned to neighboring vintners for additional advice.

For their tasting room, the Barrs chose a peaceful setting. Perched on a low hill overlooking thirty-seven acres of Cabernet Sauvignon, the cottagelike building sports a cut stone facade and matching chimney. In front are a shaded picnic area and small block of head-pruned Primitivo, a Zinfandel relative that the Barrs selected for its spicy characteristics. Visitors enter the tasting room through custom nine-foot-tall alder double doors. Inside, the fourteen-foot vaulted ceiling lends a spacious airiness to the thousand-square-foot room. Persian rugs add color to the polished concrete floor, and a fireplace graces one corner. White walls provide a neutral background for work by local artists. From behind the granite bar, Tealy greets guests, her voice revealing just a hint of the family's native New Orleans.

The Barrs farm fifty-one acres of grapes, primarily Cabernet Sauvignon planted in 1999 by the property's previous owners. They grafted about ten acres to Malbec, Petit Verdot, and Albariño—some of the first Albariño in the region. The family's sustainable farming techniques include composting the winery's solid waste, reclaiming its wastewater, using owl boxes, and planting cover crops to protect the soil. In 2008 the Barrs planted three hundred Tuscan variety olive trees at the back of the property and in 2013 bottled their first estate cold-pressed extra-virgin olive oil.

Barr Estate Winery
6950 Union Rd.
Paso Robles, CA 93446
805-835-7653
info@barrestatewines.com
barrestatewines.com

Owners: Greg and Tealy Barr.

Location: 7 miles east of downtown Paso Robles.

Appellation: Paso Robles.

Hours: 11 a.m.–5 p.m. Friday–Sunday, or by appointment.

Tastings: $10 for 5 wines (applicable to purchase). Reservations requested for 8 or more guests.

Tours: By appointment.

The Wines: Albariño, Cabernet Sauvignon, Grand Finale (port-style dessert wine from Portuguese varietals), Jubilado (red Bordeaux blend), Malbec, Malbec Rosé, Petit Verdot, Petite Sirah.

Specialties: Cabernet Sauvignon, Malbec, Petit Verdot, Malbec Rosé, Albariño.

Winemakers: Greg Barr; Signe Zoller, consultant.

Annual Production: 2,000 cases.

Of Special Note: Picnic area. Winery is pet friendly. Rotating art exhibit on view in tasting room. Estate-grown olive oil available for purchase. Reserve Petit Verdot, Reserve Cabernet Sauvignon, and Reserve Petite Sirah available in tasting room only.

Nearby Attractions: Barney Schwartz Park (lake, picnic areas); Estrella Warbird Museum (restored military aircraft, memorabilia).

CALCAREOUS VINEYARD

CALCAREOUS VINEYARD
3430 Peachy Canyon Rd.
Paso Robles, CA 93446
805-239-0289
info@calcareous.com
calcareous.com

OWNERS: Dana Brown,
Erika Messer.

LOCATION: 3 miles west of
downtown Paso Robles.

APPELLATION: Paso Robles.

HOURS: 11 A.M.–5 P.M. daily.

TASTINGS: $10 for 6–8 wines.

TOURS: By appointment.

THE WINES: Bordeaux blend,
Cabernet Sauvignon,
Chardonnay, Petit Verdot,
Pinot Noir, Rhône blend,
Roussanne, Syrah, Viognier,
Zinfandel.

SPECIALTIES: Tres Violet
(Mourvèdre, Syrah,
Grenache blend), Lloyd
(Bordeaux-style blend).

WINEMAKER:
Jason Joyce.

ANNUAL PRODUCTION:
10,500 cases.

OF SPECIAL NOTE: Picnic
area with tables; bocce
ball court. Food-and-wine
pairing available weekends,
noon–3 P.M. Gift shop
stocks books, wine acces-
sories, and light snacks.

NEARBY ATTRACTION:
Paso Robles City Park
(site of festivals, summer
concerts, farmers' market).

The owners and staff at Calcareous Vineyard invite visitors to come for the wine and stay for the sense of place, a compelling offer of liquid art and authentic landscape. Named after the chalky soil that distinguishes its west side *terroir,* the hilltop winery features a thick lawn dotted with tables and chairs, an official bocce ball court, and a stunning panorama of hills, oaks, and sky. With glass walls made of accordion doors that can be collapsed to admit air and even more light, the tasting room serves as a fitting showcase for both the lush wines and the site's considerable attributes.

Inside, stone pillars contrast with the mahogany hues of the open-beamed ceiling and tasting bar, and the open floor space allows plenty of room for mingling with other tasters, browsing the display tables, or catching the endless view. The tasting room opened in 2008, after a smaller one in the winery proved to be too limited, and was named Lloyd's Lookout, in honor of Lloyd Messer, the winery's visionary cofounder. Messer was a traveling man whose Iowa-based beer and wine distributing business frequently brought him

to Paso Robles, where he enjoyed rubbing elbows with area winemakers and dreaming about a different kind of life. When he sold his business to become a grape grower in the late 1990s, he asked his daughter, Dana Brown, to join him as a partner. Brown, who had started a wine distributorship after college, was ready for a career change after having her first child. She caught her dad's enthusiasm, sold her business, and headed west.

In 2000 the pair purchased nearly eight hundred acres of land, but not before securing fruit for the winery's 1999 debut vintage of Chardonnay and Pinot Noir. Eager to move ahead, they planted a twenty-five-acre vineyard and continued to make wine at neighboring facilities with purchased fruit, until opening their own winery in March 2006. When their vineyard began producing, they dedicated the Calcareous label to their estate program. Twisted Paso, the winery's second label, is wryly named for its focus on fruit approachability and Paso *terroir.*

Since Lloyd's unexpected death in May 2006, Brown and her sister, Erika, have shouldered the details of the business. The sisters continue to build the brand and celebrate his daring dream. Atop a chunk of calcareous soil in a flowerbed beside the tasting room, they have placed a bronzed pair of Lloyd's old work boots, a loving tribute to the man whose vision started it all.

Caliza Winery

While contemplating what to call the western Paso Robles winery they founded in 2006, Carl and Pam Bowker discovered the word *caliza*, Spanish for "limestone," a fittingly evocative name for the sixty-acre property they purchased off Highway 46 West where Anderson Road dead-ends into ranchland. In this part of the Central Coast, the seismic equivalent of what created France's Rhône Valley took place, transforming previously undersea terrain into limestone hills hospitable to grapes. Although the Bowkers grow small amounts of Spanish Tempranillo and Italian Primitivo on their site's twenty acres of vineyard, most of the rest is planted to Rhône varietals: nearly half to Syrah, with smaller amounts of Grenache, Viognier, Roussanne, and Mourvèdre.

For the Bowkers, the path to becoming "Rhône Rangers," as North American champions of Rhône varietals dub themselves, began not in France, but in Italy. In late 2001, then running a San Francisco Bay Area–based business that supplied plants and flowers to trade-show vendors, the couple joined a food-and-wine tour of Tuscany and became enchanted by the passion and "cool lifestyle," as Carl describes it, of the region's winemaking families. Upon returning home, Carl enrolled in viticulture and enology classes at Napa Valley College. In 2002 he and Pam acquired a Cabernet Sauvignon vineyard in the Peachy Canyon district of western Paso Robles and in late 2003 added the Anderson tract.

Though Carl made Caliza's earliest wines from purchased grapes, he believes in crafting wines "from the ground to the bottle." Dissatisfied with the first harvest from the existing Anderson vineyard, the Bowkers had its vines ripped out. Their trellised replacements were spaced more tightly to stress them into producing more richly flavored fruit. This substantial financial investment seemed even more risky when the U.S. economy crashed in late 2008 just as the debut Caliza vintages came to market. A few months later, however, the 2006 Syrah won the award for best red wine at the prestigious 2009 *San Francisco Chronicle* Wine Competition.

No one-hit wonder, Caliza continues to earn high praise, but the tasting experience here is convivial and unpretentious. The Bowkers often pour their wines themselves, among them the flagship Azimuth, Carl's variation on a traditional Châteauneuf-du-Pape red blend, and share their enthusiasm for Rhône blends. In fine weather you can sit outside near the huge pine tree the couple accommodated when building the tasting room. On hot days the Kissin' Cousins Viognier-heavy white blend provides the perfect antidote, as does the Rosé.

Caliza Winery
2570 Anderson Rd.
Paso Robles, CA 93446
805-237-1480
info@calizawinery.com
calizawinery.com

Owners: Carl and Pam Bowker.

Location: About 3 miles northwest of Hwy. 46 West exit off U.S. 101.

Appellation: Paso Robles.

Hours: 11 A.M.–4:30 P.M. Friday–Sunday, and by appointment.

Tastings: $15 for 5 wines.

Tours: None.

The Wines: Azimuth (Grenache, Syrah, Mourvèdre), Cohort (Syrah, Petite Sirah, Grenache), Companion (Cabernet Sauvignon, Syrah), Kissin' Cousins (Viognier, Grenache Blanc, Roussanne), Pink (rosé of Syrah and Grenache), Primitivo, Sidekick (Roussanne, Viognier), Sympatico (Tempranillo, Grenache), Syrah, Viognier.

Specialties: Rhône-style blends.

Winemaker: Carl Bowker.

Annual Production: 2,000 cases.

Of Special Note: Owners are often in tasting room. Winery is pet friendly. Outdoor picnic area. Annual events include Vintage Paso: Zinfandel and Other Wild Wines (March), Paso Robles Wine Festival (May), Harvest Wine Weekend (October). Most wines available only in tasting room.

Nearby Attraction: Templeton Park (events including weekly farmers market and summer concerts).

CASTORO CELLARS

CASTORO CELLARS
1315 N. Bethel Rd.
Templeton, CA 93465
805-238-0725
888-DAM-FINE
tastingroom@castoro
cellars.com
castorocellars.com

OWNERS: Niels and
Bimmer Udsen.

LOCATION: Hwy. 46 West,
4 miles west of U.S. 101.

APPELLATION: Paso Robles.

HOURS: 10 A.M.–5:30 P.M.
daily.

TASTINGS: Complimentary
for 3 wines; $5 for 7 wines
(applicable to purchase).

TOURS: None.

THE WINES: Barbera,
Cabernet Sauvignon,
Charbono, Chardonnay,
Chenin Blanc, Gewürztra-
miner, Grenache, Malbec,
Marsanne, Merlot, Muscat
Canelli, Petit Verdot, Petite
Sirah, Pinot Grigio, Pinot
Noir, Roussanne, Sauvignon
Blanc, Syrah, Tempranillo,
Viognier, Zinfandel.

SPECIALTIES: Zinfusion
(blend of estate Zinfandel),
Tango (white blend),
Annual Anniversary Blend
(red blend), Brut Champe-
noise sparkling wine.

WINEMAKER: Tom Myers.

ANNUAL PRODUCTION:
30,000 cases.

OF SPECIAL NOTE: Extensive
gift shop with Tunisian
ceramic dishware, logo wear,
gift items, and gourmet
snacks. Two picnic areas.
Two stages for summer
and winter concerts. Win-
ery is pet friendly. Trenta
Anni, Tango, and many
single-varietal wines available in tasting room only.

NEARBY ATTRACTION:
Jack Creek Farms
(demonstration gardens,
pick-your-own produce,
May–November).

One of the region's oldest wineries, Castoro Cellars was established in 1983, the year Paso Robles became an appellation. Husband-and-wife founders Niels and Bimmer Udsen displayed a signature sense of fun when they named their enterprise Castoro—the Italian translation of Niels's childhood moniker, Beaver—and coined the incomparable tag line: "Dam Fine Wine!"

Raised in Ventura, California, Niels often traveled with his Danish father to Denmark, where he met Bimmer, the daughter of his father's best friend. Bimmer's father, a home winemaker, shared his craft with Niels, sparking a passion in the young man. Shortly after earning a degree in agricultural business from Cal Poly San Luis Obispo in 1981, Niels married Bimmer and took a cellar worker job at Estrella River Winery, one of Paso Robles's earliest modern wineries. At Estrella, Niels met and worked under his mentor, winemaker Tom Myers. In 1991 Myers joined Castoro as winemaker, a position he still holds.

In 1994 the Udsens bought the Templeton property and remodeled the existing structure, adding an exterior faux finish and red tile roof to reflect a Mediterra-nean style. The 2,500-square-foot tasting room features a beamed ceiling, a wood-burning fireplace built from local limestone, and a mahogany tasting bar. A rattan settee with beige cushions faces the fireplace, and tables and display cases brim with wine accessories and gourmet snacks. Located in an adjoining room is an auxiliary tasting bar built from oak barrel staves and topped with granite.

The Udsens farm seven vineyards throughout the Paso Robles appellation and source fruit for their production from 750 acres of estate vineyards. Of that, 350 acres are farmed organically and certified by California Certified Organic Farmers. The rest are SIP certified under the Central Coast Vineyard Team's Sustainability in Practice program, which fosters sustainable farming and business practices. The winery bottles some twenty different offerings, including its flagship Zinfusion (a select blend of estate Zinfandel), proprietary red blends, and a wide range of white wines.

The family-friendly winery welcomes tasters to linger under the hundred-foot-long pergola lead-ing to the tasting room and enjoy the parklike grounds. Two scenic picnic areas overlook thirty-five-year-old Zinfandel vines in the estate's Cobble Creek Vineyard. In summer, the winery hosts concerts on a shaded outdoor stage that have included such acts as Tower of Power, Dave Mason, and Karla Bonoff. Acoustic winter concerts are held indoors in the 3,000-square-foot Events Center, located opposite the tasting room. The center also houses rotating exhibits of original work by local artists.

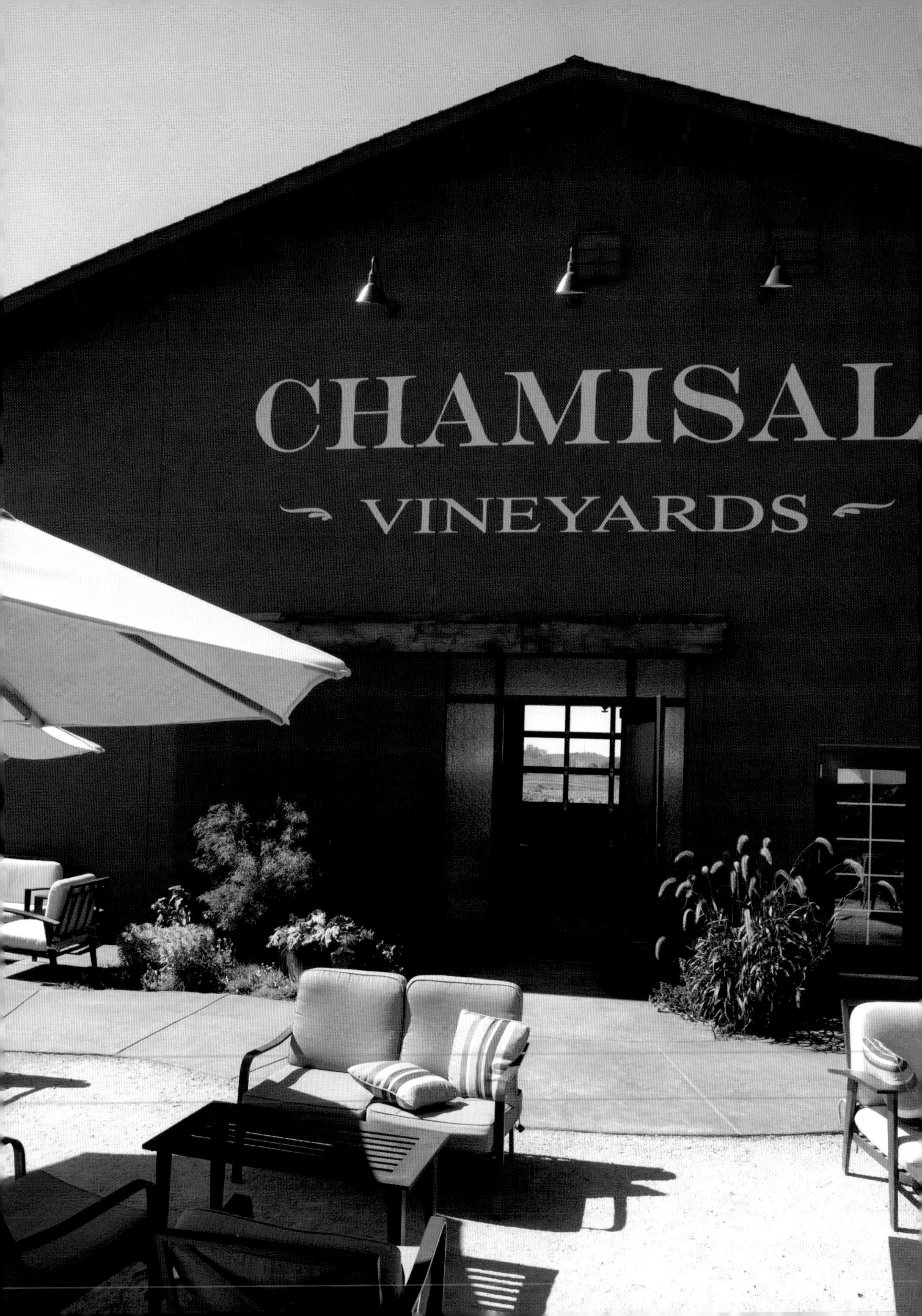
CHAMISAL
VINEYARDS

CHAMISAL VINEYARDS

From February through March, dense stands of chamise, a native evergreen shrub with fragrant white flowers, cover more than seven million acres of California's hills with a magnificent blanket of "snow." These brushlands, also called *chamissal*, thrive in calcareous, clay-rich, nutrient-poor soil on dry, rocky slopes—the same challenging topography that encourages Pinot Noir and Chardonnay vines to produce flavorful grapes.

In 1973 the Goss family planted Chamisal Vineyards, the first vineyard in the Edna Valley appellation, in the chamise-speckled Santa Lucia Mountain foothills. In 1994 new owners purchased the property and renamed it  Domaine Alfred. They recognized the ideal conditions for growing quality Pinot Noir and Chardonnay, including the cool marine air flowing through the valley, and planted a range of clones—genetically exact copies of rootstocks known to thrive in these conditions—whose fruit hangs longer on the vine and thereby develops rich, complex flavors. Crimson Wine Group acquired the estate in 2008 and restored the original name, Chamisal, to honor the vineyard's history.

Today Chamisal Vineyards cultivates eighty-five acres planted with twenty-five different clones of five varietals, mostly Pinot Noir and Chardonnay. Each clonal selection matches a particular microclimate on the estate and expresses a subtle difference in flavor. All fieldwork is done by hand, and the estate's environmentally friendly farming methods incorporate sustainable principles. Winemaker Fintan du Fresne strives to make wines that reflect the vineyard's complex character—a blend of fruity and savory he calls "Chamisal Spice." He grew up in New Zealand, where his father, a well-known wine journalist, exposed him to the enology world, and where he studied ways in which geology affects *terroir*. He especially appreciates the estate's unusually broad range of clonal varieties, which gives him many different options for creative blends.

Chamisal wines are poured in the rustic-chic tasting room in the original winery from the 1970s—a lofty barn, perched on a knoll amid the vineyards. Outdoors, a patio and picnic area provide alternative spaces for tasting and picnics. Tables custom made by a local artisan encourage visitors to enjoy the pastoral vineyard and mountain views.

CHAMISAL VINEYARDS
7525 Orcutt Rd.
San Luis Obispo, CA 93401
805-541-9463
866-808-9463
tastingroom@chamisal
vineyards.com
chamisalvineyards.com

OWNER: Crimson Wine Group.

LOCATION: 9 miles south of downtown San Luis Obispo and 2 miles south of Biddle Ranch Rd.

APPELLATION: Edna Valley.

HOURS: 10 A.M.–5 P.M. daily.

TASTINGS: $15 for Classic Flight. $25 for Estate Flight.

TOURS: None.

THE WINES: Chardonnay, Grenache, Pinot Gris, Pinot Noir, Syrah.

SPECIALTIES: Estate and Califa Edna Valley Chardonnay and Pinot Noir, plus small-lot, cool-climate Grenache and Syrah.

WINEMAKER: Fintan du Fresne.

ANNUAL PRODUCTION: 20,000 cases.

OF SPECIAL NOTE: Pet-friendly outdoor picnic area. Special events include Roll Out the Barrels (June); vineyard concert (mid-July); Lobsterfest (first weekend in August); Harvest Celebration (first weekend in November). Pinot Gris, Grenache, Syrah, and reserve and select Pinot Noir available only in tasting room.

NEARBY ATTRACTIONS: Mission San Luis Obispo de Tolosa; San Luis Obispo County Historical Museum and other historic buildings in downtown San Luis Obispo; Pismo State Beach.

DERBY WINE ESTATES

DERBY WINE ESTATES
525 Riverside Ave.
Paso Robles, CA 93446
805-238-6300
800-659-0820
info@derbywineestates
.com
derbywineestates.com

OWNERS: Ray and Pam
Derby.

LOCATION: .5 mile east of
downtown Paso Robles.

APPELLATION: Paso Robles.

HOURS: 11 A.M.–5 P.M. daily.

TASTINGS: $10.

TOURS: By appointment;
no charge.

THE WINES: Albariño,
Cabernet Sauvignon,
Marsanne, Merlot, Petite
Sirah, Pinot Gris, Pinot
Noir, Roussanne, Syrah,
Viognier, and Zinfandel.

SPECIALTIES: Implico (red
Bordeaux blend), sparkling
Pinot Noir rosé.

WINEMAKER:
Tiffinee Vierra.

ANNUAL PRODUCTION:
4,000 cases.

OF SPECIAL NOTE: Historic
photos on display docu-
ment the original building.
Food-and-wine pairings by
appointment. Shaded patio
for picnics. Tasting room
located in historic building.

NEARBY ATTRACTIONS:
Downtown Paso Robles,
Paso Robles City Park
(site of festivals, summer
concerts, farmers market),
Paso Robles Pioneer
Museum (historical
displays, vintage vehicles
and tractors).

Before moving to San Luis Obispo County in 1991, Ray and Pam Derby maintained a small Southern California avocado orchard as a hobby. But it wasn't until after selling their automotive fastener business that their casual interest in farming blossomed into a major postretirement project. In 1998 the couple bought a 632-acre cattle ranch, complete with avocado orchard, near San Simeon. Recognizing viticulture's pivotal role in the region, they did extensive research before planting 65 acres of grapes on the ranch. Despite chilly weather and marauding zebras from nearby Hearst Ranch, the coastal Derbyshire Vineyard produces exquisite Pinot Noir.

In 2001 the Derbys bought Laura's Vineyard, a warm-climate site seven miles northeast of their downtown tasting room. Planted in 1977, the vineyard provided fruit for Estrella River Winery, the region's earliest modern-day winery. The purchase included a coveted winemaking bond, or license, and to keep it active, the Derbys began making wine in 2005, after seven years of growing grapes to sell. In 2006 the Derbys acquired a 127-acre property with a mature vineyard that they expanded to 64 acres. This, the Derby Vineyard, is in the famed Templeton Gap. The Derbys grow twenty-four grape varieties and sell 95 percent of their highly regarded fruit to renowned California producers. The remaining 5 percent is reserved for their own label.

In 2010 the Derbys bought the Farmers Alliance building, which is among the significant historic landmarks in Paso Robles. The 1922 Art Deco warehouse boasts an eighty-two-foot-tall, cupola-topped tower, the city's tallest structure. The couple spent three years meticulously restoring the cupola and finishing the exterior with salmon-colored stucco to match the original. On the south end, they equipped a crush pad and adapted a former conveyor tunnel to accommodate hoses for pumping juice into tanks inside the winery. On the north end, a new outdoor patio was furnished with a welcoming fire pit, bistro tables, and market umbrellas. The Derbys repurposed the interior to include an 11,000-square-foot winery with a barrel room and a 700-square-foot, L-shaped tasting room. The white Caesarstone quartz countertop reflects light from glass shelves and illuminated glass panels behind the bar, infusing the room with Roaring Twenties glamour. The new winery and tasting room opened in 2014.

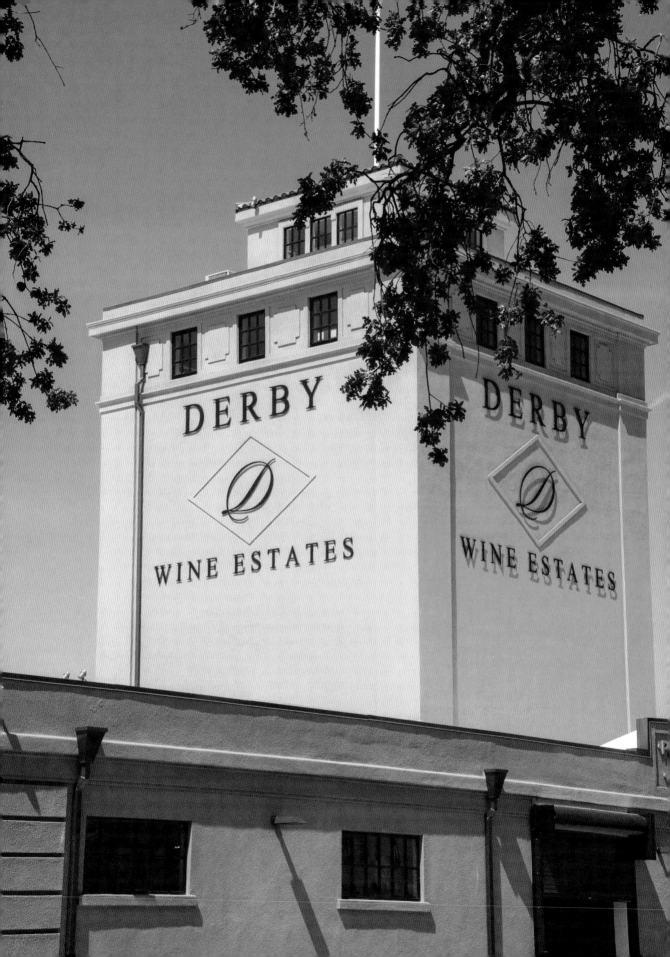

EBERLE WINERY

In Paso Robles, the name Eberle conjures two iconic figures: pioneering winemaker Gary Eberle, who planted the region's first Syrah vines and helped establish Paso Robles as a premier wine-growing region, and the small statue of a wild boar, the mascot of Eberle Winery. *Eberle* means "small boar" in German, and images of wild boars appear on the winery logo. A bronze boar, cast by Baroque master Pietro Tacca in 1620, sits at the winery entrance. *Il Porcellino*, a replica of the marble boar that once stood in the Uffizi in Florence, invites visitors to rub its snout and toss coins in the fountain beneath its feet—a Florentine tradition said to bring good luck.

This good fortune is most readily apparent at the expansive oak tasting bar, where samples of Eberle wines are poured at no charge, a rarity in the region. It also comes in the form of free guided tours through the 1,700 square feet of caves beneath the visitor center. The complimentary tours and tastings reflect Gary Eberle's firm belief in educating visitors about all aspects of winemaking so they form a personal connection to the bottles of wine they enjoy at the table.

Eberle's passion for wine, Cabernet Sauvignon in particular, developed when he was a doctoral student in cellular genetics at Louisiana State University. He decided he would rather be a winemaker and transferred to the enology doctoral program at U.C. Davis. In the early 1970s, he and his professors made a few pilgrimages to Paso Robles to collect soil samples, and their research pinpointed Paso Robles as an area of great grape-growing promise. He moved there to cofound Estrella River Winery (now Meridian) and worked as head winemaker for nearly a decade. He planted Syrah vines in 1974—the first in the United States since the repeal of Prohibition—and was the first Paso Robles winemaker to make a 100 percent Syrah wine. Eberle officially established his own label and winery partnership in 1982, purchasing sixty-five acres just a few miles west of Estrella River Winery. That year he released his flagship wine, the 1979 Cabernet Sauvignon. He also helped establish the Paso Robles appellation and completed a utilitarian cedar winery building.

The Eberle estate vineyard now produces Cabernet, Chardonnay, and Muscat Canelli grapes exclusively for Eberle wines. Eberle also has a partnership in nearby Mill Road and Steinbeck vineyards, which retain 20 percent of the harvest for Eberle wines and sell the remainder to other vintners. Over the decades, Eberle wines have earned more than three hundred gold medals, many of which are on display in the spacious California ranch–style visitor center overlooking one of Paso Robles's oldest and most legendary vineyards.

EBERLE WINERY
3810 Hwy. 46 East
Paso Robles, CA 93446
805-238-9607
tastingroom@eberlewinery.com
eberlewinery.com

FOUNDER: Gary Eberle.

LOCATION: 3.5 miles east of U.S. 101.

APPELLATION: Paso Robles.

HOURS: 10 A.M.–5 P.M. daily in winter; 10 A.M.–6 P.M. daily in summer.

TASTINGS: Complimentary for 5 wines.

TOURS: Free guided cave tours every hour daily. VIP tours ($25) include reserve tasting; reservations required.

THE WINES: Barbera, Cabernet Sauvignon, Chardonnay, Muscat Canelli, Sangiovese, Syrah, Viognier, Zinfandel.

SPECIALTIES: Vineyard-designated Cabernet Sauvignon and Syrah, vintage Port.

WINEMAKER: Ben Mayo.

ANNUAL PRODUCTION: 30,000 cases.

OF SPECIAL NOTE: Extensive wine caves available for touring. Quarterly guest chef dinners in caves. Picnic deck overlooking vineyard; on-site bocce ball court. Gift shop offering ceramic ware, wine and food books, gourmet foods, and clothing. One-third of the winery's production, including library reserve wines, available only in tasting room.

NEARBY ATTRACTIONS: Paso Robles City Park (site of festivals, summer concerts, farmers' market); Estrella Warbird Museum (restored military aircraft, memorabilia).

EOS

EOS
2300 Airport Rd.
Paso Robles, CA 93446
805-591-8050
800-249-9463
tastingroom@eosvintage
.com
eosvintage.com

OWNER: William Foley II.

LOCATION: 3 miles east
of Hwy. 46 East exit off
U.S. 101.

APPELLATION: Paso Robles.

HOURS: 10 A.M. – 5 P.M. daily.

TASTINGS: $5 for 6 wines.
$10 for 6 reserve wines.

TOURS: None.

THE WINES: Cabernet
Sauvignon, Chardonnay,
Moscato (late harvest),
Muscat Canelli, Petite Sirah,
Port, Rosé, Sauvignon Blanc,
Sauvignon Blanc (late har-
vest), Sémillon (botrytised),
Syrah, Zinfandel.

SPECIALTIES: Dessert wines
including Tears of Dew Late
Harvest Moscato, Zinfandel
Series.

WINEMAKER: Paul Warson.

ANNUAL PRODUCTION:
18,000 cases.

OF SPECIAL NOTE: Spacious
outside picnic area. Winery
is pet friendly. Snack items
available. Extensive gift
shop. Private wine-tasting
lunch by appointment.
Annual events include
Vintage Paso: Zinfandel and
Other Wild Wines (March),
Harvest Wine Weekend
(October), Holiday Open
House (December). Many
wines available only in tasting room.

NEARBY ATTRACTIONS: Paso
Robles City Park (site of
festivals, summer concerts,
farmers market); Estrella
Warbird Museum
(restored military aircraft,
memorabilia).

Ownership changes at wineries usually trigger dramatic expansion to recoup financing costs, but when Foley Family Wines purchased Eos in 2010 from the original propri-etors, the opposite transpired. Reversing the "something for everyone" philosophy that characterized the pre-Foley era, production was slashed from more than a quarter-million cases to fewer than 18,000 as the eastern Paso Robles winery repositioned itself as a purveyor of accessible wines exceptional for both their quality and their affordability.

Founded in the mid-1980s and named for the Greek goddess of the dawn, Eos underwent swift changes, says current winemaker Paul Warson, who honed his craft at two elite Napa Val-ley wineries, Ch. Potelle and  Trefethen, before heading south to recast the wine program at another Foley acquisition, the Santa Ynez–based Firestone label. There was no thought, of dropping the Tears of Dew Late Harvest Moscato, the most high-profile offering at the time. Indeed, dessert wines remain such an Eos staple that guests can sample a flight solely of sweet vintages. The reconceived Eos also showcases what War-son describes as the Paso Robles AVA's core strength: deep, rich red wines, most notably the estate Cabernet Sauvignon, a Petite Sirah, and a Zinfandel that reflect the region's climate and terrain. White wines include Chardonnay, Sauvignon Blanc, and a Roussanne-Viognier blend.

Except for its sole estate wine, the Cabernet, made from grapes grown in the gravelly five acres outside the tasting room, Eos sources grapes from other Foley wineries and top-rated producers from around California. With seven Zinfandels crafted from grapes grown in Paso Robles, the Napa Valley, Sonoma County's Dry Creek and Russian River valleys, and Amador County in the Sierra Nevada Gold Country, Eos provides guests the opportunity to experience the diverse ways this adaptable varietal expresses itself across the state.

A two-level terraced picnic area, bordered by a ledgestone wall and complete with a faux-stone mini-waterfall, fronts the tasting room building. Once visitors are inside, two things immediately capture the attention: the three-story, oak-beamed ceiling and the gift shop so large and fancifully stocked that it's a destination, especially during the Christmas holidays. Even nonshoppers may find themselves intrigued by the latest wine accessories and the artworks and crafts fashioned from recycled oak barrels and other wine-related components. Local gourmet foods sold here include gelato and sorbetto, along with addictive almond brittle. All these treats pair splendidly with the sweet Eos wines.

Grey Wolf Cellars and Barton Vineyards

Two bronze wolves howl at the entrance to Grey Wolf Cellars, a midcentury farmhouse that the Barton family converted into a tasting room in 1996. Originally from Bakersfield, California, Shirlene and Joe Barton Sr. often passed the house while traveling to their vacation home in Cambria. Stopping along the way to taste wine, they befriended the proprietors of such local producers as Peachy Canyon Winery and Castoro Cellars. A carpenter, Joe Sr. built homes, and Shirlene taught high school, but with their two children nearly grown, they were eager for a lifestyle change. Joe Sr. wanted to make wine, so while working construction at Justin Vineyards, he traded labor for grapes. He sought advice from local vintners and learned his craft through trial and error. When friends of the Bartons bought a vineyard on Paso Robles's eastside in 1992, the couple partnered with them and began making wine commercially.

The Bartons purchased the farmhouse property in 1995 after their partners lost interest in the eastside vineyard and sold the property. Keen to join the family business, the Bartons' son, Joe, studied at Cal Poly San Luis Obispo and graduated with a fruit science degree. In 1998 Joe Sr. passed away suddenly. Vowing to keep his dream alive, Shirlene took charge of the tasting room, and Joe stepped in as winemaker. Since then Joe has developed a hands-on vinicultural style that showcases the fruit's intrinsic characteristics. He relies on native yeasts to trigger fermentation, which he feels results in more flavorful wines. Joe sources fruit from the seven-acre estate vineyard planted beside the farmhouse in 1998. He also buys grapes from local growers, maintaining relationships forged by his father. The Grey Wolf Cellars portfolio is composed entirely of rich, blended red wines, while a second label, Barton Family Wines, represents what Joe considers stylistic departures. Offerings include Viognier, Sauvignon Blanc, and reserve-vineyard designated reds.

Ancient oak, pine, and olive trees shade the clapboard tasting room. A bilevel patio offers wrought iron tables and chairs, and seating at a wooden bar that overlooks the Barton's estate Zinfandel vines. Inside the 1,200-square-foot tasting room, a vaulted ceiling, exposed oak beams, and original oak floor evoke a rustic country bungalow. Hanging photographs include images of Barton family ancestors, as well as the property's homesteaders. A fireplace of local Adelaida stone is set into one wall, and the opposite wall is paneled with pine planks salvaged from century-old pickle barrels. Behind the oak tasting bar, the kitchenlike space includes an oak farmhouse-style table, 1930s-era stove, and matching refrigerator for chilling white wines.

Grey Wolf Cellars and Barton Vineyards
2174 Hwy. 46 West
Paso Robles, CA 93446
805-237-0771
howl@greywolfcellars.com
bartonfamilywines.com

Owners: Shirlene and Joseph Barton.

Location: 2.5 miles west of U.S. 101 on Hwy. 46 West.

Appellation: Paso Robles.

Hours: 11 a.m.–5:30 p.m. daily.

Tastings: $7 for 7 wines (applicable to purchase).

Tours: None.

The Wines: Cabernet Sauvignon, Chardonnay, Chenin Blanc, Sauvignon Blanc, Viognier, Zinfandel.

Specialties: Zinfandel, Cabernet Sauvignon.

Winemaker: Joe Barton.

Annual Production: 3,500 cases.

Of Special Note: Wines made in small lots of 50 to 400 cases each, with limited distribution. Most wines available in tasting room only.

Nearby Attractions: Templeton Park (events including weekly farmers market and summer concerts); Jack Creek Farms (demonstration gardens, pick-your-own produce, May–November).

HALTER RANCH VINEYARD

HALTER RANCH VINEYARD
8910 Adelaida Rd.
Paso Robles, CA 93446
805-226-9455
info@halterranch.com
halterranch.com

OWNER: Hansjörg Wyss.

LOCATION: 9 miles north-west of the intersection of Hwy. 46 West and Vineyard Dr.

APPELLATION: Paso Robles.

HOURS: 11 A.M.–5 P.M. daily.

TASTINGS: $10 for 6 or 7 wines (applicable to purchase).

TOURS: 11 A.M., noon, and 1 P.M. Saturday and Sunday, weekdays by appointment.

THE WINES: Cabernet Sauvignon, Grenache Rosé, red and white Rhône blends, Syrah, Viognier.

SPECIALTIES: Ancestor (Bordeaux-style blend), Côtes de Paso (red Rhône-style blend), Côtes de Paso Blanc (white Rhône-style blend.

WINEMAKER: Kevin Sass.

ANNUAL PRODUCTION: 12,000 cases.

OF SPECIAL NOTE: Picnic snacks available on-site. Picnic area located in garden outside tasting room. Winery is pet friendly. Annual summer solstice dinner. Single-variety wines available only in tasting room. A registered champion coast live oak, one of the two largest specimens in the U.S., stands in the middle of one vineyard.

NEARBY ATTRACTIONS: Mt. Olive Organic Farm (tours, olive oil tasting, bakery, lunch menu); Pasolivo Olive Oil (olive oil tasting, specialty salts, vinegar, and lotions, picnicking).

Located on a thousand acres just west of Paso Robles, Halter Ranch Vineyard has been part of a working ranch since 1880. With its farmhouse, mature orchards, and vintage outbuildings, it continues to offer a taste of old California. At the end of the driveway, the restored Victorian farmhouse stands among towering oaks, cottage gardens, and sixty-year-old olive trees. The two-story house, with its red roof and period detailing, glows pale yellow in the dappled shade. Nearby, an enlarged carriage house serves as the tasting room. Inside, open beams enhance the impression of an elegant cabin fitted with a cork floor and curved cherrywood tasting bar. Broad windows are set into one side, and clear glass in a gabled end admits extra light. Two sets of french doors open onto a patio beside Las Tablas Creek. Beyond the tasting room, a collection of nineteenth-century barns and grain silos remains as evidence of a long agricultural tradition.

A covered bridge spanning the creek leads to the estate's magnificent 34,000-square-foot winery, completed in 2011. Clad in cedar siding, the winery resembles the old barns on the ranch, but with a chalet-like flavor in keeping with owner Hansjörg Wyss's Swiss roots. Copper gutters flash in the sun, and portions of the exterior walls are faced with Adelaida stone taken from the property and cut on-site. The state-of-the-art facility stands on a hill 1,600 feet in elevation and embraces a number of green features, including a cooling system that automatically draws in chilly night air. It also boasts a gravity flow system that gently transports juice throughout the winery, yielding exceptional wine. Underground, 20,000 square feet of recently constructed caves offer cool, naturally insulated space for aging wine-filled barrels.

Just beyond the winery's landscaped beds of lavender and drought-tolerant grasses grow Cabernet Sauvignon, Grenache, and Syrah, part of the estate's 280 acres of grapes. The vineyards are planted to twenty different varieties, many of which are farmed with no supplemental irrigation. To help control pests, chickens roam the rows by day, returning at dusk to their mobile coop, which is equipped with a solar-powered gate. The vineyards are all Sustainability in Practice (SIP) certified, having met standards set by the Central Coast Vineyard Team in areas such as water conservation, energy efficiency, and labor relations. Primarily Rhône- and Bordeaux-style blends, the wines are 100 percent estate grown and also SIP certified. The Estate Reserve red blend, called Ancestor, is named for a massive, centuries-old live oak growing near the vineyard, a living reminder of the property's long history and a harbinger of its promising future.

HammerSky Vineyards

Built for a Mennonite minister and his family, the gleaming white house at HammerSky Vineyards dates to 1904. When Douglas Hauck and his wife, Kim, bought the fifty-acre property in 2007, they converted the colonial-style gem into a luxurious inn. Despite the home's age, its crisp black shutters, second-floor balcony, and cropped boxwood hedge reveal a contemporary aesthetic. The couple oriented windows to incorporate views of a centuries-old valley oak, affectionately known as Uncle Dan, and erected a post-and-beam Yankee barn behind the house for winery events.

The Haucks farm twenty-five acres of grapes at HammerSky Vineyards, which they named for their two young sons, Hamilton and Skyler. Planted in 1997, the vines grow in soil that compares favorably with that of France's Bordeaux region. A combination of shale, clay loam, and calcareous sandstone, the soil harbors moisture, encouraging the vines to root deeply, and imparts a balanced minerality to the finished wine.

While Kim runs the inn, Doug is involved in all aspects of the wine business, including marketing, vineyard management, and blending stylish wines that he considers couture for the senses. A man of diverse interests, Doug earned a business degree from the University of Southern California, a film degree from the University of California, Los Angeles, and, in 1988, a doctorate of dental surgery from San Francisco's University of the Pacific. He taught dental courses at USC, ran a successful practice in Beverly Hills for two decades, and has enjoyed side careers as a movie producer and Internet entrepreneur. Doug continues to maintain his practice in Orange County, where he counts sports, music, and film celebrities among his clients.

The Haucks' eclectic sense of style is especially evident in the tasting room, which stands at the edge of a parklike lawn dotted with white oaks and picnic tables. The clean lines and smooth, steel-troweled walls of the snow-white structure create a bold impact amid the rural setting. The building, a melding of the refined esthetics of both Doug and Kim Hauck, is just under a thousand square feet and includes an airy space for wine tasting, as well as a barrel room splashed with red and black accents. Tall windows and glass doors admit natural light, while allowing sweeping views of the Merlot vines that border the lawn and café-style seating on the patio. A rough-hewn rectangular table doubles as a tasting bar. To provide at-a-glance information about the wine, Doug created Sensory Integrated Profiling, a visual graph based on the tasting criteria of swirl, sniff, sip, and savor. Individual profiles appear on the back of each bottle, adding a contemporary twist to the old-fashioned pleasures of wine tasting.

HammerSky Vineyards
7725 Vineyard Dr.
Paso Robles, CA 93446
805-239-0930
tastingroom@hammersky.com
hammersky.com

Owners: Doug and Kim Hauck.

Location: 5 miles northwest of the intersection of Hwy. 46 West and Vineyard Dr.

Appellation: Paso Robles.

Hours: 11 A.M.–5 P.M. Thursday–Sunday.

Tastings: $10 for 3–5 wines; $15 for 2 reserve wines.

Tours: None.

The Wines: Cabernet Franc, Cabernet Sauvignon, Merlot, Petit Verdot, Zinfandel.

Specialties: Bordeaux-centric blends, Cabernet Sauvignon, Merlot, Zinfandel.

Winemaker: Doug Hauck.

Annual Production: 2,600 cases.

Of Special Note: Wines are 90 percent estate grown. Live music and food on spring and summer weekends. Property includes a 4-bedroom inn open year-around. Red Handed (100 percent Merlot) available in tasting room only.

Nearby Attractions: Mt. Olive Organic Farm (tours, olive oil tasting, bakery, lunch menu); Pasolivo Olive Oil (olive oil tasting, specialty salts, vinegar, and lotions, picnicking).

HEARST RANCH WINERY

HEARST RANCH WINERY
442 SLO San Simeon Rd.
San Simeon, CA 93452
805-467-2241
info@hearstranchwinery
.com
hearstranchwinery.com

OWNERS: Jim and Debi
Saunders; Steve Hearst.

LOCATION: 9 miles north of
Cambria on Hwy. 1.

APPELLATION: Paso Robles.

HOURS: 11 A.M.–5 P.M.
daily October–April;
11 A.M.–6 P.M. daily
May – September.

TASTINGS: $10 for 6 wines
(applicable to purchase).

TOURS: None.

THE WINES: Cabernet Franc,
Cabernet Sauvignon,
Chardonnay, Late Harvest
Zinfandel, Malbec, Merlot,
Petite Sirah, Rosé, Tempra-
nillo, Zinfandel.

SPECIALTIES: Point Barrel
Select Cuvée (Bordeaux-
style red blend), Three
Sisters Cuvée series (red and
white Rhône-style blends),
Malbec, Tempranillo, Cab-
ernet Franc.

WINEMAKERS: Jim Saunders,
Guillaume Fabre.

ANNUAL PRODUCTION:
12,000 cases.

OF SPECIAL NOTE: Tasting
room located inside historic
building shared with Sebas-
tian's Deli. Picnic area with
view of San Simeon Bay and
Hearst Castle. Food-and-
wine pairings by appoint-
ment. Events include
Harvest Winemaker Dinner.
Hearst Ranch grass-fed beef
served at deli.

NEARBY ATTRACTIONS: Hearst
Castle; William Randolph
Hearst Memorial State
Beach; elephant seal rookery
at Piedras Blancas; boat
tours to see migrating
whales.

Although it sits across coastal Highway 1 from an architectural icon and shares its lofty pedigree, the tasting room of Hearst Ranch Winery strikes a disarmingly down-home pose. The compact space is inside a converted circa 1852 whaling store that also houses a deli and the local post office. The gracefully warped fir plank flooring and carefully selected artifacts associated with the nearby Hearst Castle and adjoining Hearst Ranch immediately catch the eye. Front and center are vintage crates marked "W.R. Hearst San Simeon" that once held fine art shipped to the famous newspaper magnate William Randolph for the estate he christened "La Cuesta Encantada" (The Enchanted Hill). The copper-topped tasting bar provides unexpected delights, including horseshoes bent to hold women's purses and restored barn siding from old ranch buildings. Two nineteenth-century whaling room's earlier function.

The visual appeal extends beyond the room as well. W.R.'s architect, Julia Morgan, designed the Mission Revival–style warehouse across the street to store his substantial art collection; its large archway frames views of San Simeon Bay. Depending on the time of year, dolphins or migrating whales can be seen plying the waters.

With all the historical and natural diversions, the Hearst Ranch wines could easily end up mere afterthoughts, but they're decidedly not, having already earned this young enterprise accolades that include winery of the year at the 2011 Central Coast Wine Competition. As with so many things Hearst, how they came to carry that storied name involves a good yarn. In 2009 Jim Saunders, a Paso Robles grape grower whose construction firm built several local wineries, attended a charity auction and placed a winning bid on a behind-the-scenes tour of Hearst Castle. His host: W.R.'s great-grandson Steve Hearst. The two hit it off, and before the year ended they had become partners, producing wines made from Malbec, Petite Sirah, Petit Verdot, Syrah, and Tempranillo grapes from Saunders Vineyard, and fruit from other sources, including Chardonnay, Cabernet Sauvignon, and Zinfandel, purchased from top Central Coast growers. The wines' names all bear a Hearst connection: the Julia Rosé, for example, honors the castle's architect.

W.R. once wrote to Morgan, "There's money in wine grapes. We ought to grow 'em." The two never did, but in 2013 Steve Hearst fulfilled his great-grandfather's wish by planting a small block of Malbec at the fog line near a mile-plus-long pergola W.R. built. These nascent vines enjoy an extraordinary view—westward to the Pacific—and if the experiment yields equally exceptional wines, more plantings will surely follow.

HEARTHSTONE ESTATE

From its hilltop vantage point, Hearthstone Estate offers sweeping westward views of neighboring farms and the Santa Lucia Mountains. Mature pines and live oaks shade the wooded site, and a weathered fertilizer wagon in the parking area hints at the region's agrarian history. Opened in 2009, the earth-toned tasting room sports a concrete crush pad and two arched redwood doors that reveal the building's original function as a small private winery. Stones excavated from the property and set into the lower portion of the exterior wall give the structure the look of a mountain house.

topiaries flank three glass into the tasting room. Above the winery's sinuous logo, a rising from an unseen hearth. concrete flooring meets cor- matches the front of the tasting At the entry, spiral juniper panels, two of which open the panels, a fanlight bears Gaelic-spirited swirl of smoke Inside the square room, gray rugated tin wainscoting that bar. Behind the oak-topped bar, wine bottles and a vineyard scene are mounted on a curved partition of similar corrugated tin.

In fair weather, visitors can sample wine on the patio in front of the tasting room, an ideal spot to enjoy spectacular sunsets. A transparent windbreak shelters the patio from cool ocean air funneled through a series of notches—collectively known as the Templeton Gap—in the Santa Lucia Mountains. The breezes moderate temperatures on the hill and in the vineyard, located eight miles northeast. The forty-acre vineyard grows at 1,400 feet elevation and in shallow calcareous soil, conditions that limit vine production to light crops of small grapes with highly concentrated flavors.

Owner Hoy Buell, a horticulturist and graduate of Cal Poly San Luis Obispo, is a cofounder of Greenheart Farms, one of the nation's largest wholesale nurseries. He had been propagating vines for other growers when, in 1999, he heeded the siren call to plant his own vineyard. Buell sustainably farms twenty different grape varieties, selects about half of the crop for his estate wines, and sells the rest to local winemakers. Given the wide variety of grapes and their limited yields, winemaker Paul Ayers makes small lots of unique blends. Harvest is done clone by clone, and each two-ton batch of fruit is fermented separately. A twenty-eight-year veteran, Ayers honed his craft at a number of the region's pioneer wineries, including Estrella River Winery and Castoro Cellars. When not tending the wines, which are made at a neighboring facility, he often can be found helping out in the tasting room or chatting with visitors over a glass of one of his blends.

HEARTHSTONE ESTATE
5070 Vineyard Dr.
Paso Robles, CA 93446
805-238-2544
info@hearthstonevineyard
.com
hearthstonevineyard.com

OWNER: Hoy Buell.

LOCATION: 2 miles north-west of the intersection of Hwy. 46 West and Vineyard Dr.

APPELLATION: Paso Robles.

HOURS: 11 A.M.–5 P.M. Thursday–Monday.

TASTINGS: $10 for 7 wines (applicable to purchase).

TOURS: None.

THE WINES: Cabernet Franc, Cabernet Sauvignon, Grenache, Mourvèdre, Petite Sirah, Pinot Noir, Roussanne, Sangiovese, Syrah, Tempranillo, Viognier, Zinfandel.

SPECIALTIES: Rhône- and Bordeaux-style blends, small-lot proprietary blends.

WINEMAKER: Paul Ayers.

ANNUAL PRODUCTION: 2,000 cases.

OF SPECIAL NOTE: All wines are estate grown and sold primarily out of the tasting room. Educational seminars quarterly.

NEARBY ATTRACTIONS: Mt. Olive Organic Farm (tours, olive and olive oil tasting, bakery, lunch menu); Pasolivo Olive Oil (olive oil tasting, specialty vinegars, salts, and lotions, picnicking).

J. LOHR VINEYARDS & WINES

J. LOHR VINEYARDS & WINES
6169 Airport Rd.
Paso Robles, CA 93446
805-239-8900
prwinecenter@jlohr.com
jlohr.com

OWNERS: Jerry Lohr, Steve Lohr, Cynthia Lohr, and Lawrence Lohr.

LOCATION: 6 miles northeast of downtown Paso Robles.

APPELLATION: Paso Robles.

HOURS: 10 A.M.–5 P.M. daily.

TASTINGS: No fee, except for the Cuvée Series trio of wines and the limited-production wines ($5), available Friday, Saturday, and Sunday only.

TOURS: None.

THE WINES: Cabernet Sauvignon, Chardonnay, Grenache, Merlot, Mourvèdre, Petite Sirah, Pinot Noir, Riesling, Sauvignon Blanc, Syrah, Valdiguié, Viognier, Zinfandel.

SPECIALTIES: Cuvée Series (Bordeaux-style blends), Gesture series (Rhône-inspired blends and varieties).

WINEMAKERS: Jeff Meier, director of winemaking; Steve Peck, red winemaker.

ANNUAL PRODUCTION: 1.5 million cases.

OF SPECIAL NOTE: Cookbooks, culinary and wine accessories, and items crafted by local artisans sold in tasting room. Rhône-inspired Gesture series available in tasting room only. The original J. Lohr San Jose Wine Center is open daily, 10 A.M.–5 P.M.

NEARBY ATTRACTIONS: Estrella Warbird Museum (restored military aircraft); Centennial Park (playground, picnic area, walking paths).

Raised on a South Dakota farm, Jerry Lohr enjoyed successful careers as a civil engineer and custom home builder. A passion for wine, however, drove him back to his agricultural roots. In the late 1960s, Lohr began scouting California's Central Coast for vineyard sites. He took viticulture and enology classes at U.C. Davis and in 1973 planted a 280-acre vineyard in Monterey County. A year later he opened a winery in San Jose that produced popular wines at affordable prices. Stimulated by the challenges of the wine industry, Lohr planted a vineyard near Sacramento and purchased a thirty-five-acre vineyard in Napa Valley. Determining that Paso Robles would be ideal for growing red grapes, he planted Cabernet Sauvignon vines about six miles north of the city in 1986 and became one of Paso Robles's viticultural pioneers. Two years later, Lohr built a winery and barrel room near his vineyard.

Confident in the region's potential for producing superior fruit, Lohr eventually planted more than 3,000 acres of vines in the Paso Robles appellation. It was a heavy commitment, but with the 1989 launch of his J. Lohr Estates wines featuring all-estate fruit, Lohr elevated his label to a new level of quality. In 2002 he introduced the heralded J. Lohr Cuvée Series, a trio of blended red wines made in the styles of the Bordeaux regions of Pauillac, St. Emilion, and Pomerol. Debuting in 2009, the Gesture series of Rhône-inspired wines reflects the distinctive microclimates of western Paso Robles. Both series are produced in limited quantities.

Jerry Lohr has long been active in the wine industry. He has been recognized for his many contributions, most recently in 2011, when he received the prestigious Lifetime Achievement Award from the California Association of Winegrape Growers. Lohr, with his winegrowing and farming expertise, and his experienced winemaking team—Jeff Meier, director of winemaking, who has been with the winery for thirty-one years, and red winemaker Steve Peck—enjoy a productive partnership whose consistency and attention to detail have brought acclaim to the J. Lohr portfolio of wines.

Lohr's three grown children, Steve, Cynthia, and Lawrence, hold executive positions in the family business and share ownership with Jerry. Eldest son Steve was recently named chairman and CEO. In 2009 the Lohrs unveiled a three-acre solar tracking array located behind the Paso Robles winery, the largest winery-based solar array of its kind in North America. At the J. Lohr Paso Robles Wine Center, a wraparound veranda set with teak tables and chairs offers visitors views of the Cabernet Sauvignon vines that Lohr planted a quarter of a century ago.

JUSTIN VINEYARDS & WINERY

Cattle dominated the rangeland in 1981 when Justin Baldwin purchased 160 acres west of Paso Robles. With funds for a modest venture, he planted 72 acres of Bordeaux-type vines. At the time, his was the westernmost vineyard in a region with only nine wineries. Baldwin, a well-traveled investment banker, had enjoyed many fine vintages with clients and boldly resolved to make wines comparable to the first growths of Bordeaux. In 1987, four years after he helped establish the Paso Robles appellation, Baldwin debuted his flagship wine. A Bordeaux-style blend, it was called Isosceles, in reference to its three constituents of Cabernet Sauvignon, Cabernet Franc, and Merlot.

By 1996 Baldwin had built a state-of-the-art winery complex on the property. A year later, at the London International Wine and Spirits Competition, the 1994 Isosceles was named the world's best blended red Bordeaux-style wine, a coup that put Justin Vineyards—and Paso Robles—on the international wine map. In 2003 the winery completed 18,000 square feet of caves for storing 5,000 barrels. At the deepest part of the caves, 120 feet belowground, lies the Isosceles Library, which is featured on winery tours. Niches in the gunite walls hold past vintages, liquid histories that track the progress of Baldwin's maturing estate vineyard. All tours include a visit to the caves.

Lying thirteen miles from the Pacific Ocean, the vineyard grows at elevations ranging between 1,200 and 1,800 feet. Farming practices include the use of nitrogen-fixing cover crops between rows and biodynamic preparations for healthy soil. In 2012, shortly after Stewart and Lynda Resnick purchased the winery, new Cabernet Sauvignon vines were planted around the tasting room.

Remodeled in 2013, the tasting room is a contemporary, 3,500-square-foot space with white walls lit by natural light spilling through glass doors and windows on three sides. Oversized square pendant lamps complement the elegant setting. In contrast, woodwork on the bar and sleek display tables bears a dark walnut finish, as does the plank floor. The U-shaped tasting bar sports a zinc top. On the west side of the tasting room, a tiered patio features teak tables and chairs shaded by white market umbrellas and sits at the edge of one of the estate's Cabernet Sauvignon vineyards. Visitors can make reservations to enjoy lunch or dinner at the winery's on-site restaurant, which serves gourmet fare and seasonal specialties. The restaurant was remodeled from six tables to eight and reoriented to provide dramatic vineyard views to the north and west, with glass doors opening onto the restaurant's inviting terrace.

JUSTIN VINEYARDS & WINERY
11680 Chimney Rock Rd.
Paso Robles, CA 93446
805-238-6932
concierge@justinwine.com
justinwine.com

OWNERS: Stewart and Lynda Resnick.

LOCATION: 13 miles north-west of intersection of Hwy. 46 West and Vineyard Dr.

APPELLATION: Paso Robles.

HOURS: 10 A.M.–4:30 P.M. daily.

TASTINGS: $10 for 5 wines. Barrel tasting ($30) 3:30 P.M. Sunday–Thursday, with reservation 48 hours in advance.

TOURS: Winery and cave tours ($20), 10 A.M. and 2:30 P.M. daily, include tasting in caves.

THE WINES: Cabernet Franc, Cabernet Sauvignon, Malbec, Merlot, Sauvignon Blanc, Syrah.

SPECIALTIES: Isosceles (Cabernet Sauvignon, Cabernet Franc, Merlot), Savant (Syrah, Cabernet Sauvignon), Justification (Cabernet Franc, Merlot), Focus (Syrah, Grenache).

WINEMAKER: Scott Shirley.

ANNUAL PRODUCTION: 100,000 cases.

OF SPECIAL NOTE: Wine seminars March–November. Tasting room stocks light snacks, books, and wine accessories. Restaurant serves dinner Tuesday–Saturday, lunch Friday–Sunday. A bed-and-breakfast inn is on-site. Private tasting and barrel sampling Monday–Thursday by appointment.

NEARBY ATTRACTION: Pasolivo Olive Oil (olive oil tasting, specialty vinegars, salts, and lotions, picnicking).

LAETITIA VINEYARD & WINERY

LAETITIA VINEYARD & WINERY
453 Laetitia Vineyard Dr.
Arroyo Grande, CA 93420
805-474-7651
888-809-VINE
laetitiawine.com

OWNER: Selim Zilkha.

LOCATION: Directly off U.S.
101, between the towns of
Nipomo and Pismo Beach.

APPELLATION: Arroyo
Grande Valley.

HOURS: 11 A.M.–5 P.M. daily.

TASTINGS: $10 for any
5 wines.

TOURS: None.

THE WINES: Brut Cuvée and
Brut Rosé sparkling wines,
Cabernet Sauvignon, Char-
donnay, Pinot Noir, Syrah.

SPECIALTIES: Estate Pinot
Noir, *méthode champenoise*
sparkling wines.

WINEMAKERS: Eric Hickey
(still wines); Dave Hickey
(sparkling wines).

ANNUAL PRODUCTION:
60,000 cases.

OF SPECIAL NOTE: Visitors
can see fully operational
press room. Five picnic
areas with umbrellas;
bocce ball court on-
site. Gift shop offering
clothing, stemware, and
books. Select Pinot Noirs
and NADIA wines from
Santa Barbara Highlands
vineyard available only in
tasting room.

NEARBY ATTRACTIONS:
Arroyo Grande Village
(Old West downtown with
historic walking tour);
Pismo State Beach (swim-
ming, hiking, camping).

The stunning views from the hilltop decks at Laetitia Vineyard & Winery rival the best on the Central Coast: a panorama of vineyards, the pastoral Arroyo Grande Valley, and the Pacific Ocean, just three miles to the west. In 1982 this gorgeous site captivated French viticulturists from Champagne Deutz, the esteemed Champagne house, who were searching for a suitable location to grow grapes and produce *méthode champenoise* sparkling wines in the United States. The viticulturalists were also impressed with the property's volcanic soils and climates, which resembled those in their native Epernay, France, and would promote high acid and minerality. They planted 185 acres to Pinot Noir, Chardonnay, and Pinot Blanc in specific sites chosen for their soil profile, exposure, and microclimate, and established Maison Deutz, a winery that quickly earned a reputation for outstanding sparkling wines.

In 1997 vineyard owner chased Maison Deutz and after his daughter. The win- sparkling wine to still wine style varieties, and experimen- potential as a premier site for Jean-Claude Tardivat pur- renamed the winery Laetitia ery's focus began to shift from production of Burgundian- tation revealed the vineyards' growing Pinot Noir. A year later, the winery was acquired by a partnership that included Selim Zilkha. In 2001 Zilkha obtained sole proprietorship of Laetitia.

Today the 1,800-acre Laetitia ranch includes 620 acres of vineyard blocks, with 430 acres devoted to Pinot Noir. Laetitia also owns a second vineyard, Santa Barbara Highlands, at a 3,200-foot elevation, sixty miles inland in the Cuyama Valley. This vineyard grows mostly Bordeaux varieties for Laetitia's NADIA portfolio of wines. The Hickey family manages nearly all day-to-day winery business. Winemaker Eric Hickey, who has worked at the winery since 1990, directs the still wine production and general operations. Eric's father, Dave Hickey, began his career at Maison Deutz in 1985. He continues the winery's French tradition by making sparkling wines in the *champenoise* method, producing bubbles during a secondary fermentation in the bottle rather than in barrels. Eric's mother, Carmen, manages the tasting room, and his brother, Dustin, helps out in the cellar.

Visitors to the casual, country-style tasting room can view the adjacent press room, which houses two rare Coquard wooden basket presses, made in France, that Dave Hickey uses to press estate-grown Pinot Noir, Chardonnay, and Pinot Blanc grapes. These are the only such presses operated in the United States. Outdoors, visitors can relax in Adirondack chairs under yellow and white umbrellas on a lawn, above the gravity-flow winery and sweeping scenes of the ocean beyond.

OPOLO VINEYARDS

Heading through the gate at Opolo Vineyards, visitors enter a viticultural wonderland anchored by an unassuming tasting room: a converted tractor barn decorated to inspire guests to relax and have fun. Famed for its loyal fans and weekend festivities, often featuring grilled delicacies—from sausage and lamb to Cevapcici, a Serbian-style roll of minced beef—this event-driven destination serves up a lively mix of food, wine, and convivial pleasure. Guests can sip wine on the covered deck while taking in the vineyard views, or they can step inside, where giant posters brighten the walls and stacked barrels share space with cases of wine. At wooden planks laid atop oak barrels, friendly staffers pour the listed wines, and then, based on each taster's preferences, suggest others from the winery's thirty-some offerings.

Opolo Vineyards owners, Rick Quinn and David Nichols, share the winemaking duties and welcome feedback from the staff, information that they feel helps them produce wines with the widest customer appeal. When evaluating potential blends, they sometimes even ask tasting room visitors to weigh in on the decision.

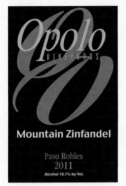

A software developer and owner of a real estate brokerage, Quinn first made wine with his family in Minnesota. He revived the tradition when he moved to Southern California, where his successes inspired Nichols, his neighbor and the proprietor of a wireless electronics firm, to take up the hobby. In 1995, when Quinn's Merlot source dried up, the dynamic businessman planted his own vineyard on the west side of Paso Robles with an eye toward supplying his home winemaking needs and selling the rest of the crop to commercial producers. That same year, Nichols bought the vineyard next to Quinn's, and the two plunged into the grape-growing business, selling their fruit to such respected Napa Valley cellars as Niebaum-Coppola, St. Supéry, Fetzer, and Hess Collection. Today they farm three hundred acres of vineyards on the west and east sides and continue to sell fruit to some of the finest wineries in the state.

In 1998 the business partners noted an industry-wide surplus of grapes and began making wine under their own label in a bid to showcase their vineyards' quality and enhance grape sales. The partners bottled some Merlot, labeling half "Merlot" and the other half "Opolo," the name of a Dalmatian Coast wine selected to honor Quinn's heritage. Believing the wines to be different, friends overwhelmingly preferred the latter, making Opolo, in Nichols's words, the "slam dunk" choice for the name of their new enterprise. Ten years and thousands of cases later, the partners have created a viticultural destination with a well-earned reputation for treating visitors to a good time.

OPOLO VINEYARDS
7110 Vineyard Dr.
Paso Robles, CA 93446
805-238-9593
sales@opolo.com
opolo.com

OWNERS: Rick Quinn, David Nichols.

LOCATION: 8 miles west of U.S. 101.

APPELLATION: Paso Robles.

HOURS: 10 A.M.–5 P.M. daily.

TASTINGS: $5.

TOURS: By appointment.

THE WINES: Albariño, Barbera, Cabernet Sauvignon, Chardonnay, Grenache, Malbec, Merlot, Mourvèdre, Muscat Canelli, Petit Verdot, Petite Sirah, Pinot Grigio, Pinot Noir, Roussanne, Sangiovese, Syrah, Tempranillo, Viognier, Zinfandel.

SPECIALTIES: Montagna-Mare (Barbera, Sangiovese blend), Mountain Zinfandel, Rhapsody (Merlot, Cabernet Sauvignon, Petit Verdot blend).

WINEMAKERS: Rick Quinn, David Nichols.

ANNUAL PRODUCTION: 40,000 cases.

OF SPECIAL NOTE: On-site bed-and-breakfast, the Inn at Opolo. Harvest grape stomp and various weekend events.

NEARBY ATTRACTION: Mt. Olive Organic Farm (tours, olive and olive oil tasting, bakery, lunch menu).

PasoPort Wine Company

PasoPort Wine Company
95 Booker Rd.
Templeton, CA 93465
805-239-2229
info@pasoportwine.com
pasoportwine.com

Owners: Steve and Lola Glossner.

Location: Off Hwy. 46 West, 4 miles west of U.S. 101.

Appellation: Paso Robles.

Hours: 11 A.M.–5 P.M. Thursday–Monday, and by appointment.

Tastings: Complimentary.

Tours: None.

The Wines: Albariño, Cabernet Sauvignon, Grenache, Merlot, Pinot Noir, port-style wines, Syrah, Tempranillo, Touriga Nacional, Zinfandel.

Specialties: Aged port-style wine, brandy, grappa, seasonal fruit liqueurs.

Winemaker: Steve Glossner.

Annual Production: 2,500 cases.

Of Special Note: Distillery on-site. Port-and-chocolate-truffle-pairing events open to the public November and May. Limited-release PasoPort sparkling wine and aged port-style wines, Per Cazo table wines, and Willow Creek brandy and spirits available in winery only.

Nearby Attractions: Templeton Park (events including weekly summer concerts); Jack Creek Farms (demonstration gardens, pick-your-own produce, May–November).

Among the first local producers to feature port-style wines, Steve and Lola Glossner founded PasoPort Wine Company in 2005. The couple decided to produce port-style wines to tap into a promising niche market and to craft a unique product from local fruit, much of it farmed without supplemental irrigation and thus possessing the quality, structure, and intense flavors required to make superior port-style wine.

With Steve as winemaker and Lola handling the marketing, the couple specializes in dessert wines made by adding brandy to fermenting grape juice, a technique that originated in Portugal. Distilled from wine, brandy contains up to 80 percent alcohol, a high concentration that stops fermentation, yielding naturally sweet wine. Port-style wines were especially popular during the 1940s, and to evoke that era, the Glossners' labels showcase images of glamorous pin-up girls. The Ruby Port is a blend of Zinfandel, Petite Sirah, and Syrah; the Violeta Port boasts a traditional blend of Portuguese grape varietals. Some components in the Angelica White and Tawny ports have been barrel aged as long as ten years.

Steve began making wine in Paso Robles in 1994 at Justin Vineyards. While there, he crafted the award-winning 1994 Isosceles, a blended red wine. In 1999 he became winemaker at Adelaida Cellars, where he helped plant Portuguese wine grapes for the winery's port-style wine program. In 2002, as director of winemaking, Steve developed Halter Ranch Vineyard's initial wine portfolio. Six years later, Steve became consulting winemaker for the Per Cazo label ("by chance" in Italian). When Per Cazo's owners moved out of the state in 2013, the Glossners bought the label, under which they bottle their table wines, which include Rhône and Bordeaux blends. With the purchase of a Holstein pot still that same year, the Glossners established Willow Creek Distilling for making brandy, as well as grappa and liqueurs. The copper still gleams beyond a viewing window in the knotty pine wall dividing the nearly nine-hundred-square-foot winery. For licensing reasons, brandy, which contains more alcohol than wine, is sampled inside the distillery area, while wines are sampled in the winery.

The softly lit winery features a bar built of reclaimed redwood slabs set atop brandy barrels. Brushed aluminum stools provide seating. Knotty pine trusses overhead and a stainless steel roll-up door reveal the utilitarian nature of the barn that the Glossners repurposed for their facility. Located at 1,200 feet elevation, the round-roof barn was built in 2000, but an exterior faux finish makes it look older. In fair weather, double doors of knotty pine are opened to connect the winery with an outdoor patio, where visitors have views of the Santa Lucia Range.

Pear Valley Vineyards

The road to winery ownership is paved metaphorically in many ways, but in the case of Pear Valley Vineyards the process was quite literal. After his youngest child left for college, owner Tom Maas eased out of his successful Southern California road construction business, purchased land in Paso Robles and San Miguel, and began growing grapes. His wife and co-owner, Kathleen, admits that she initially supported her husband's dream with reluctance, but over time the intricacies of the wine business came to fascinate her as well—so much that she now eagerly attends classes on the latest in viticultural practices, water and energy conservation, and even winery accounting. Influenced by analyses of California's drought cycles, Kathleen advocated installing a $300,000 system to recycle wastewater from the winemaking process back into the vineyards. Her prescience paid off when drought plagued the state.

A long dirt driveway winds toward the tasting room past trellised rows of vines labeled with the names of the two dozen varietals used to create Pear Valley's diverse roster. Asked why all the grape types and why every wine is estate designated, Kathleen replies with a smile that her husband's tastes are varied and that "he's a control freak, in the good sense," zealous about ensuring the quality of every drop. Tom, whose workingman's hands are his most striking feature—they helped build the winery—is also a whiz at fixing machinery and is just as apt to be tinkering in the fields or the winery as toiling in the business office. He leaves the day-to-day winemaking, though, to Jared Lee, whom the Maases met at the custom crush facility in Paso Robles where they made wine before their winery was built.

Sixty-five tractor-trailers delivered the sand-colored stone used to erect the monumental Pear Valley winery and tasting room complex, inspired by European castles and châteaus the Maases researched before construction commenced. Light streams in the tasting room's tall paned windows and french doors, which provide pastoral views extending for miles. Double-thick stone walls and the high ceiling supported by broad finished fir beams hung with contemporary tapestries heighten the sense of comfortable splendor.

A tasting at Pear Valley provides an opportunity to sample lesser-known varietals such as Albariño and Aglianico, along with the flagship red, Distraction. The Bordeaux blend earned its name a few years back after Kathleen, irked by Tom's incessant remixing to achieve the perfect flavor profile, asked if he'd deign to tear himself away from his "distraction" to handle another matter. The name serves as a reminder of the single-mindedness of purpose that has helped Pear Valley thrive.

Pear Valley Vineyards
4900 Union Rd.
Paso Robles, CA 93446
805-237-2861
info@pearvalley.com
pearvalley.com

Owners: Tom and Kathleen Maas.

Location: 3 miles southeast of Hwy. 46 E and Union Rd.

Appellation: Paso Robles.

Hours: 11 a.m.–5 p.m. daily.

Tastings: $5 for 6 wines.

Tours: By appointment.

The Wines: Aglianico, Albariño, Cabernet Franc, Cabernet Sauvignon, Charbono, Chardonnay, Chenin Blanc, Grenache, Malbec, Muscat Blanc, Orange Muscat, Petite Sirah, Pinot Noir, Rosé, Sauvignon Blanc, Syrah, Viognier, Zinfandel.

Specialties: Belle Fin (late-harvest Cabernet Franc), Bom Final (Port-style dessert wine), Distraction (Bordeaux blend), Inspiration (Grenache, Syrah, Mourvèdre).

Winemaker: Jared Lee.

Annual Production: 5,500 cases.

Of Special Note: Old-world-style architecture. Shaded outdoor picnic area with views. Annual events include Vintage Paso: Zinfandel and Other Wild Wines (March), Paso Robles Wine Festival (May), Harvest Wine Weekend (October). Evening concerts third Friday of month. All wines made from 100 percent estate fruit and available only in tasting room.

Nearby Attractions: Barney Schwartz Park (lake, picnic areas); Estrella Warbird Museum (restored military aircraft, memorabilia).

PENMAN SPRINGS VINEYARD

PENMAN SPRINGS VINEYARD
1985 Penman Springs Rd.
Paso Robles, CA 93446
805-237-7959
penmansprings@gmail
.com
penmansprings.com

OWNERS: Carl and
Beth McCasland.

LOCATION: 2.5 miles east
of Hwy. 46 East.

APPELLATION: Paso Robles.

HOURS: 11 A.M.–5 P.M.
Thursday–Monday.

TASTINGS: $5 (applicable
to purchase).

TOURS: None.

THE WINES: Cabernet
Sauvignon, Meritage,
Merlot, Muscat Blanc, Petit
Verdot, Petite Sirah, Syrah,
fortified wine.

SPECIALTIES: Cabernet
Sauvignon "Old Block,"
Meritage "Artisan Cuvée,"
Penman Reserve, Petite
Sirah.

WINEMAKER: Larry Roberts.

ANNUAL PRODUCTION:
2,400 cases.

OF SPECIAL NOTE: Picnic
area. Penman Pantry
stocks books, local condiments, one-of-a-kind jew-
elry, and handmade goat
milk soap. Late-harvest
and fortified wines available only at tasting room.

NEARBY ATTRACTIONS:
Barney Schwartz Park
(lake, picnic areas);
Estrella Warbird Museum
(restored military aircraft,
memorabilia).

Penman Springs Vineyard stands on a broad rise overlooking vineyards, oak savannas, and sculpted hills. Although the rural scenery and country solitude suggest a more remote spot, the winery is located just three miles east of downtown Paso Robles. A short driveway curves past the winery's vineyard and ends at the tasting room, which faces blocks of Petite Sirah and gnarled Cabernet Sauvignon vines.

To encourage visitors to take in the spectacular view while enjoying a picnic lunch, owners Beth and Carl McCasland have placed concrete tables and benches beside the tasting room. Entering the white board-and-batten build- 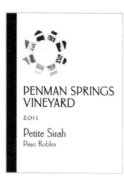 ing, visitors find a homey space, complete with an upright piano, a pellet-burning stove, and a table spread with a jigsaw puzzle in progress. As in the early days when Paso Robles tasting rooms were usu- ally staffed by their owners, Beth is often behind the bar. She believes in treating tasters as if they were guests in her home and occasion- ally pairs Penman Springs wines with artisan breads, meats, and cheeses. After calling out a cheer- ful greeting, she ensures that tast- ings are relaxed, educational, and fun. Opened in 2000, the simple tasting room features a cathedral ceiling that lends elegance to the welcoming space. Wine competition ribbons line the walls, and the well-stocked Penman Pantry holds grape seed and olive oils, vinegars, and chocolate sauces, as well as locally made goat milk soap.

The McCaslands purchased what Carl calls their "garden" in 1996. The forty-acre property included sixteen acres of established grapevines. Doing much of the work himself, Carl replanted more than half of the original vines and expanded the vineyard to thirty-one acres, following sus- tainable agricultural principles. He installed a variety of trellis systems and continues to manage the grapevine canopies to allow sunshine and warm air to ripen the grapes. Inspiration for this approach came from Dr. Richard Smart's seminal book *Sunlight Into Wine*.

In 1998 the McCaslands hired Larry Roberts as their winemaker and launched the Penman Springs Vineyard brand. Roberts designed the label bearing the image of a distinctive color wheel created from shards of glass by Beth's architect brother. The McCaslands' first crush consisted of Merlot, Cabernet Sauvignon, Muscat Blanc, and purchased Chardonnay. With the production from new vines, they have expanded the line to include Syrah, Petite Sirah, Meritage, occasional Petit Verdot, and fortified dessert wines. The couple continues to work closely with Roberts to craft the wines, which are 100 percent estate grown.

POMAR JUNCTION VINEYARD & WINERY

In the late 1880s, the Templeton area was called *el pomar*, Spanish for "the orchard." By 1925, its rolling hills blossomed with some of the largest almond plantings in the world. Today, as vineyards replace the orchards, the area remains quiet, rural, and seemingly remote. A weathered red water tank stands near the intersection of El Pomar Drive and South El Pomar Road, the crossroads that inspired the Merrill family to name their winery Pomar Junction. At the winery's entrance, a wooden water tank and a green, nineteenth-century grain wagon mark the long driveway, which is lined with eighty-year-old almond trees. Resting in their shade are antique agricultural essentials, including a wooden almond

hauler.

Dana and Marsha Merrill, and their son, Matthew, represent eight generations of farming on the Central Coast. For thirty years, the family has grown wine grapes and managed vineyards for wineries, such as Robert Mondavi. As a charter member of the Central Coast Vineyard Team in the 1990s, Dana helped develop the Sustainability in Practice (SIP) certification program, which fosters sustainable agricultural and business practices by evaluating such elements as water and energy conservation, and labor relations.

In 2002 the Merrills bought the 130-acre Pomar Junction property and planted 91 acres to nearly a dozen different grape varieties. In 2008 the vineyard received SIP certification. The wines, also SIP certified, are made in a warehouse-style winery, built near the vineyard in 2011. Eager to showcase the region's warm hospitality, the Merrills converted a 1920s-era farmhouse on the property into a tasting room. The cottage features redwood arbors and a back deck, as well as a patio with garden beds and a trickling fountain. Inside, a welcoming hodgepodge of rooms has been added on over the years. A well-used brick fireplace graces what was once the living room, where amiable staffers pour wine at a copper-topped bar rescued from an 1880s-vintage Paso Robles saloon. Red oak floors and knotty pine cabinets in the kitchen are original to the house.

Out front, a mature elm tree towers over a lawn dotted with redwood picnic tables, and the driveway ends at a white clapboard shed built in the early 1920s for hulling almonds. Beyond the shed, a retired red boxcar and cupola caboose rest on a length of rail. The abbreviated train honors the Southern Pacific Railroad, which reached Templeton in 1887, as well as Marsha's grandfather, who was an engineer with the line. Picnic tables nearby afford sweeping vineyard views and a comfortable spot for enjoying the historic farmstead, a reminder of bygone days that live on at this inviting family winery.

POMAR JUNCTION VINEYARD & WINERY
5036 S. El Pomar Rd.
Templeton, CA 93465
805-238-9940
info@pomarjunction.com
pomarjunction.com

OWNERS: Dana and Marsha Merrill, Matt and Nicole Merrill.

LOCATION: 6 miles east of the intersection of U.S. 101 and Vineyard Dr.

APPELLATION: Paso Robles.

HOURS: 11 A.M.–5 P.M. daily.

TASTINGS: $5 for 5 wines.

TOURS: Winery tours on request.

THE WINES: Cabernet Sauvignon, Chardonnay, Grenache Blanc, Late Harvest Viognier, Merlot, Pinot Noir, Roussanne, Sparkling Wine, Syrah, Syrah Rosé, Viognier, Zinfandel.

SPECIALTIES: Reserve Cabernet Sauvignon, Train Wreck (red blend of Cabernet Sauvignon, Petite Sirah, Syrah, and Zinfandel), GSM (Rhône blend).

WINEMAKER: Jim Shumate.

ANNUAL PRODUCTION: 9,000 cases.

OF SPECIAL NOTE: Winery offers horse-drawn carriage tours of the vineyard. Once a month, April through October, Train Wreck Friday ($10, 5:30–8:30 P.M.) features live music. Wine accessories and gift items sold in tasting room.

NEARBY ATTRACTIONS: Templeton Park (events including weekly summer concerts, Saturday farmers' market); Jack Creek Farms (demonstration gardens, pick-your-own produce, May–November).

SEXTANT WINES

SEXTANT WINES
PASO ROBLES:
2324 Hwy. 46 West
Paso Robles, CA 93446

SAN LUIS OBISPO:
1653 Old Price Canyon Rd.
San Luis Obispo, CA 93401
805-542-0133
866-833-9643
concierge@sextantwines
.com
sextantwines.com

OWNERS: Craig and Nancy
Stoller.

LOCATION: Paso Robles:
1 mile west of U.S. 101.
San Luis Obispo: 6.5 miles
southeast of downtown.

APPELLATION: Paso Robles.

HOURS: Paso Robles:
10 A.M.–5 P.M. daily.
San Luis Obispo: 10 A.M.–
4 P.M. Monday–Friday,
10 A.M.–5 P.M. Saturday
and Sunday.

TASTINGS: $10 for 5 wines
in both tasting rooms.

TOURS: By appointment.

THE WINES: Cabernet
Sauvignon, Chardonnay,
Pinot Noir, Zinfandel.

SPECIALTIES: Cabernet
Sauvignon, Zinfandel, red
Rhône-style blends.

WINEMAKER: Steven Martell.

ANNUAL PRODUCTION:
15,000 cases.

OF SPECIAL NOTE: Both tasting rooms are pet friendly
and have patios for picnics.
Menu at San Luis Obispo
gourmet deli includes
seasonal specialties and box
lunches. Tannat, cult-style
X series, Night Watch,
Portolan, Kamal, Genoa,
and Petite Sirah available in
tasting rooms only.

NEARBY ATTRACTIONS: Paso
Robles: Jack Creek Farms
(demonstration gardens,
pick-your-own produce).
San Luis Obispo: Pismo
Beach Monarch Butterfly
Grove.

When Craig and Nancy Stoller founded Sextant Wines in 2004, they hosted tastings at their RBZ Vineyard in Templeton and poured wine samples from the back of a pickup truck. It was fitting to launch the business from a vineyard, because in 1977 Craig's father had founded Sunridge Nurseries, one of the nation's largest suppliers of grapevine stock. To provide propagation material for the nursery, Craig and Nancy installed the 114-acre RBZ Vineyard in 2002 and named it for the types of grapes planted: Rhône, Bordeaux, and Zinfandel.

Upon joining his father's business in 1991, Craig knew he would make wine. Having recently graduated from Cal Poly San Luis Obispo with an ornamental horticulture degree, he delighted in touring customers' vine- yards and tasting their wares. In 1995 Craig and Nancy married, and within a year Craig had begun making wine in the couple's garage. To reflect their love of the ocean, they named their wines Sextant, after an ancient celestial navigation

device. Working out of rented spaces, the Stollers, both natives of Kern County, California, grew their business slowly. In 2007 they purchased the twelve-acre MacGregor Vineyard in Edna Valley, one of the valley's earliest plantings, dating to 1974. Two years later, they opened a tasting room in historic Edna Hall, built in 1908 as a hotel and general store. The corrugated tin structure, six miles southeast of downtown San Luis Obispo, stands within sight of MacGregor Vineyard, on the old Edna townsite. The Stollers equipped Edna Hall with a copper-topped bar, hung art on the white-paneled walls, and put in a gourmet deli.

In need of a permanent home, the couple transformed a bilevel steel building in Paso Robles into a second tasting room, with a winery on the floor below. The elegant facility, opened in 2012, features an entryway arch that evokes a Venetian bridge. The nearly circular arch is clad with local Adelaida stone and giant fossilized clams unearthed on the property. Two ten-foot-tall doors are bordered with Peruvian walnut and planked in Canary teak. Inside the 2,000-square-foot tasting room, aquamarine light pulses from behind teak veneer ceiling panels cut out to resemble undulat-ing seaweed. Madagascan labradorite granite tops the bar, and pewter nautilus shells serve as dump buckets. Four windows on each side of the room provide views into the barrel and tank rooms below. In keeping with the nautical theme, wine names include Wheelhouse (their flagship Zinfandel) and Portolan, a red Rhône-style blend named for a medieval nautical chart. Fruit is sourced from nearly 450 acres of estate vineyards located in San Luis Obispo and Monterey counties.

Siot and Rotta Winery

Zinfandel and Cabernet vineyards plunge precipitously toward the tasting room at Siot and Rotta Winery. The gnarly vines, "head trained" old Europe–style rather than trellised, look like mini Joshua trees, arms outstretched haphazardly. Only the widely spaced rows lend order to this tumultuous tableau, whose origins date back to the tectonic shifts that elevated the ocean floor and created the Santa Lucia Range.

The sense of sea change prevails once again at Siot and Rotta Winery, purchased in 2013 by Jason Shorrock. An oenophile and history buff with experience marketing spirits at Moet Hennessey USA and wines at Justin Vineyards & Winery, Shorrock saw in Rotta (*row-tuh*) a chance to restore luster to one of the Central Coast's oldest vineyard properties. Intrigued by the original owner,

Adolph Siot (*sigh-yot*), who planted Shorrock decided to add a reserve founder. Given that Siot was a new winemaker seems apropos: Jeff earned his master's degree in viticulture of Bordeaux. A Bordeaux blend, inaugural Siot lineup, also slated Sauvignon, a Rhône-style red, and

Zinfandel grapes here in the 1800s, tier of wine to honor the winery's Frenchman, Shorrock's choice for Branco, also previously of Justin, culture and enology at the University—Branco's specialty, will anchor the to include Chardonnay, Cabernet a cold-climate Syrah.

To his credit Shorrock has embraced Rotta Winery's legacy and retained the name as a subsidiary brand. In recent years, it turned out respectable Zinfandels and a dessert sherry, heavy on the caramel notes, called Black Monukka. During the 1960s and 1970s, the winery gained notoriety for the "Rotta Run" made by students from the nearby Cal Poly San Luis Obispo to pick up jugs of Zinfandel before hitting local surfing beaches. Black Monukka survives as a wine and a cocktail mixer, and vintage Zin bottles from the beach-party era can be seen in the tasting room, a casual, country space with a ceiling made of redwood reclaimed from old Rotta fermenting tanks. Tastings also take place on a vineyard-view patio edged by water-worn limestone embedded with whalebone and other sea fossils.

Shorrock had the Siot logo designed to incorporate a timepiece showing seven o'clock for good luck. As if to forecast more changes to come, a few months after arriving, Branco lopped off 60 percent of the Zinfandel grapes in one vineyard, hoping to intensify the flavor of the remaining fruit, slated for the winery's flagship Zinfandel, Osso Balena Vineyard Zinfandel (*osso balena* is Italian for "whalebone"). Branco's willingness to challenge past practice and Shorrock's respect for history and tradition bode well for this winery that's gone back to the future to reinvent itself.

Siot and Rotta Winery
250 Winery Rd.
Templeton, CA 93465
805-237-0510
siotwine.com

Owner: Jason Shorrock.

Location: 2.3 miles west of U.S. 101, off Las Tablas Rd.

Appellation: Paso Robles.

Hours: 10:30 a.m.– 5:30 p.m. daily.

Tastings: $10 for at least 5 wines (applicable to purchase).

Tours: $15 (with tasting), includes history of winery and Paso Robles appellation and visit to wine cellar.

The Wines: Cabernet Sauvignon, Chardonnay, Grenache, Mourvèdre , Petite Sirah, Rosé, Roussanne, Syrah, Zinfandel.

Specialties: Rotta Black Monukka dessert wine, Osso Balena Vineyard Estate Zinfandel, Siot Bordeaux and Rhône blends.

Winemaker: Jeff Branco.

Annual Production: 20,000 cases.

Of Special Note: Historic buildings and vintage equipment near tasting room. Shaded patio and outside tasting area. Winery is pet friendly.

Nearby Attractions: Templeton Park (events including weekly summer concerts); Jack Creek Farms (demonstration gardens, pick-your-own produce, May–November).

SUMMERWOOD WINERY

SUMMERWOOD WINERY
2175 Arbor Rd.
Paso Robles, CA 93446
805-227-1365
info@summerwoodwine
.com
summerwoodwine.com

OWNERS: Fukae family.

LOCATION: 1 mile west of
U.S. 101.

APPELLATION: Paso Robles.

HOURS: 10 A.M.–6 P.M. daily
in spring and summer;
10 A.M.–5 P.M. daily in fall
and winter.

TASTINGS: $10 for 5 wines.

TOURS: By appointment.

THE WINES: Cabernet
Sauvignon, Grenache,
Marsanne, Syrah, Viognier,
Zinfandel.

SPECIALTIES: Rhône- and
Bordeaux-style blends.

WINEMAKER: Mauricio
Marchant.

ANNUAL PRODUCTION:
2,500 cases.

OF SPECIAL NOTE: Newly
renovated nine-room
inn, with executive chef,
on-site. Picnic lunches
may be pre-ordered from
inn. Biannual winemaker
dinners on-site. Quarterly
wine-and-food-pairing
events ($40). Live music
on patio in summer and
fall. Zinfandel port-style
wine released each Decem-
ber. Gift shop with logo
wear, wine accessories,
gift items, and gourmet
snacks. All wines available
in tasting room only.

NEARBY ATTRACTIONS:
Templeton Park (events
including weekly farmers
market and summer con-
certs); Jack Creek Farms
(demonstration gardens,
pick-your-own produce,
May–November).

Ideally located, SummerWood Winery is often the first stop for travelers exploring wine country along Highway 46 West. The facility's wisteria-draped entryway, towering trees, and white clapboard tasting room evoke a lush country estate, making it a charming gateway to the popular westside wine trail. SummerWood Winery specializes in premium Rhône- and Bordeaux-style wines crafted in small lots. Regardless of the grape variety, winemaker Mauricio Marchant handles the fruit with a gentle touch. He destems and cold-soaks the grapes to extract color and flavor, never crushing the berries prior to fermentation. Marchant sources fruit from estate vineyards

growing beside the winery, which is located in the famed Templeton Gap. Here, afternoon breezes off the Pacific Ocean mitigate the high summer heat by cooling the grapes and helping to balance fruit acidity. In 2013 one estate vineyard block was replanted to eight different grape varieties, including white Rhône-type Grenache Blanc. Each variety will yield a small lot of about 150 cases of select wine. Marchant also buys high-quality fruit from other westside growers, such as Denner, Hearthstone, and Alta Colina vineyards. Many of these vineyards are located at elevations between 1,200 and 1,700 feet, an environmental factor that enhances the depth and complexity of fruits' flavor profiles.

SummerWood Winery is owned by businessman Kesao Fukae and his family, of Osaka, Japan. During the course of his business travels, Fukae, chairman of Japan's EH Group, developed an affinity for California's wines. He dreamed of owning a winery and in 2001 traveled to Paso Robles. Captivated by the region's wine community and diverse *terroir*, he acquired the SummerWood property, which included a tasting room, winery, estate vineyard, and guest inn. Fukae named the estate after his son, Natsuki, whose name translates to "summerwood."

The landscaped grounds of the forty-five-acre property feature a garden gazebo linked to the tasting room by a grapevine-covered pergola. Double french doors open into the elegant room, which is a combination lobby, gift shop, and wine center. Exposed oak beams create a coffered ceiling, and the slate floor is inlaid with African mahogany. A brown leather sofa and two blue side chairs near the fireplace enhance the friendly, clublike atmosphere. On one wall, windows offer a view of the winery floor below, allowing visitors to watch the cellar staff at work while sampling wine at the L-shaped tasting bar. Well-trained staff members answer questions about how the wines are grown and made, and offer creative food-pairing ideas. Acting as regional ambassadors, they even visit neighboring facilities to better advise guests seeking additional tasting experiences.

TALLEY VINEYARDS

Farmers for three generations, the Talley family knows how to tend the fertile Arroyo Grande Valley land to grow a range of delectable produce—including premium wine grapes. Oliver Talley began cultivating specialty vegetables here in 1948. In the 1980s, Don Talley, his wife, Rosemary, and his son, Brian, established Talley Vineyards in the heart of the valley and acquired historic property, once part of a Mexican land grant, with a story-laden 1860s adobe residence. Don Talley recognized the potential for growing high-quality Pinot Noir and Chardonnay on the steep hillsides above the adobe and planted a small test plot with five varieties in 1982. His hunch proved correct, and the family founded Talley Vineyards and expanded the business over the years. El Rincon Adobe served as tasting room for a dozen years.

Today the Talleys continue their farming traditions along with the winemaking business. Talley Farms supplies the region with a range of vegetables and fruits. Talley Vineyards, with Brian and his wife, Johnine, at the helm, grows grapes on 190 acres of estate vineyards in the Arroyo Grande and Edna valleys, named Rincon, Rosemary's, Monte Sereno, Las Ventanas, Oliver's, and Stone Corral. Winemaker Eric Johnson, who earned a degree in wine and viticulture studies from California Polytechnic University San Luis Obispo, applies a gentle hand to reflect the *terroir* while crafting vintages in the 8,000-square-foot gravity-flow facility on the Rincon Vineyard property. Johnson's bottlings appear under two different labels. Talley Vineyards wines focus on stellar Chardonnay and Pinot Noir produced entirely from estate vineyards. Wines bearing the label Bishop's Peak reflect the distinct characteristics of various vineyard regions in San Luis Obispo County. The winery also makes Mano Tinta wines, whose proceeds support an endowment benefiting county farmworkers.

Windows in the spacious, Tuscan-style hospitality center, built in 2002, open to spectacular views of Arroyo Grande Valley and Rincon Vineyard. The center's Rincon Room exhibits photographs of the vineyards and a time line of the property's history. On display are seven tall plexiglass cylinders holding the vineyards' diverse soils, a visual way to explain the concept of *terroir*. Visitors can relax outdoors amid the lush landscaping, which includes a picnic area next to an expansive courtyard. Additional picnic areas near the winery and historic adobe overlook farm fields and Rincon Vineyard. Tours take visitors through Rincon Vineyard, the winery, and the barrel room; an expanded tour features a reserve and library tasting. The longer, in-depth estate tour includes a barrel tasting and a fascinating visit to El Rincon Adobe, whose image appears on every Talley Vineyards label.

TALLEY VINEYARDS
3031 Lopez Dr.
Arroyo Grande, CA 93420
805-489-0446
info@talleyvineyards.com
talleyvineyards.com

OWNERS: Brian and Johnine Talley.

LOCATION: 5 miles east of U.S. 101 and Arroyo Grande on Lopez Dr.; 7.5 miles south of San Luis Obispo via Orcutt Rd.

APPELLATION: Arroyo Grande Valley.

HOURS: 10:30 A.M.– 4:30 P.M. daily.

TASTINGS: $8 for 5 wines; $12–$15 for 5 reserve wines.

TOURS: Half-hour tour by appointment ($15 with tasting, $10 without). Expanded tours by appointment: Estate Tour and Tasting ($35), Barrel Tasting ($25).

THE WINES: Cabernet Sauvignon, Chardonnay, Pinot Noir, Riesling, Sauvignon Blanc, Syrah.

SPECIALTIES: Estate-grown Chardonnay and Pinot Noir.

WINEMAKER: Eric Johnson.

ANNUAL PRODUCTION: 25,000 cases.

OF SPECIAL NOTE: Gift shop with wine accessories, snacks, and condiments. Three picnic areas. Events include San Luis Obispo Vintners Association celebrations (June and November). Small-lot specialty wines, including Riesling, Sauvignon Blanc, Syrah, and Mano Tinta, available only in tasting room.

NEARBY ATTRACTIONS: Arroyo Grande Village (Old West downtown with historic walking tour); Pismo State Beach; Lopez Lake (kayaking, mountain biking, fishing).

TREANA AND HOPE FAMILY WINES

TREANA AND HOPE FAMILY WINES
1585 Live Oak Rd.
Paso Robles, CA 93446
805-238-4112
info@hfwines.com
hopefamilywines.com

OWNERS: Hope family.

LOCATION: 2 miles west of U.S. 101, just off Hwy. 46 West.

APPELLATION: Paso Robles.

HOURS: 10 A.M.–4 P.M. Thursday–Monday, and by appointment.

TASTINGS: Complimentary for 5 wines.

TOURS: By appointment.

THE WINES: Cabernet Sauvignon, Chardonnay, Grenache, Marsanne, Merlot, Roussanne, Syrah, Viognier, Zinfandel.

SPECIALTIES: Treana Red (Cabernet Sauvignon, Syrah blend); Treana White (Viognier, Marsanne blend).

WINEMAKERS: Austin Hope, Jason Diefenderfer.

ANNUAL PRODUCTION: 350,000 cases.

OF SPECIAL NOTE: The winery also bottles wine under the Austin Hope, Candor, Troublemaker, and Liberty School labels, which are available for tasting in the tasting cellar. Annual bacon-and-wine pairing event in October.

NEARBY ATTRACTION: Paso Robles City Park (site of festivals, summer concerts, farmers' market).

Pioneers of the Paso Robles wine industry, Chuck and Marlyn Hope are second-generation farmers who moved to the Central Coast in 1978. Seeking new opportunities, they left Bakersfield to plant apple trees along the Salinas River. They also planted a vineyard that included Cabernet Sauvignon. As apple sales lagged, the couple devoted their efforts to growing quality wine grapes. The vineyard was a family affair, and even their eight-year-old son Austin helped by hoeing weeds from between the vines.

By the late 1980s the Hopes were selling Cabernet Sauvignon to the renowned Caymus Vineyards in Napa Valley. They developed a close relationship with the winery's owner, Chuck Wagner, and were among the first to tap Paso Robles' potential for producing stellar red wines. The Hopes launched their debut label, Hope Family Farms, in the early 1990s, just as Chuck Hope helped organize the Paso Robles Vintners and Growers Association.

In 1994, following the family's lead, Austin took a job at Caymus Vineyards. With Wagner as a mentor, he received an in-depth wine industry education. In 1995 Austin traveled to France to learn Rhône-style winemaking. Later that year he graduated from Cal Poly San Luis Obispo with a degree in fruit science and became assistant winemaker at Hope Family Farms. In 1996 the family founded Treana Winery, a label devoted to their signature Rhône-influenced blends. Two years later, Austin was making the flagship Treana Red. In 2009 the forty-acre Hope Family Vineyard earned Sustainability in Practice certification through a program that promotes sustainable farming. That same year the family created Hope Family Wines, under which they currently make five distinct labels sold in fifty states and ten countries. To support production, the Hopes buy additional fruit from fifty local vineyards.

At the winery, Grenache vines climb wooden stakes, suggesting a vineyard in the Rhône region. Valley oaks shade the wildlife corridor that skirts the sixty-two-acre property, which includes the family's estate vineyard. Three cedar-clad buildings served as a winery and two barrel rooms until 2009, when the Hopes converted one of the barrel rooms into an elegant tasting cellar. Inside, visitors walk between wine-filled oak barrels. Dividing the 3,000-square-foot room are two curved structures forming a grand entryway into the tasting area. Built from quarter-split white oak, they resemble wine casks wrapped with steel hoops. The barrel theme repeats at the tasting counter, where the front of the zinc-topped bar is made of white oak planks fitted with steel bands. In the white wall behind the bar, a half-dozen windows of varying sizes frame vibrant oak tree and vineyard views.

VINA ROBLES

A red-roofed showplace that draws visitors from around the world, the Vina Robles hospitality center opened in 2007, ten years after its owner, Swiss entrepreneur Hans Nef, planted the first of six estate vineyards on the eastside of Paso Robles. Nef built the winery and center with a variety of events in mind—from barbecues and concerts to banquets and conferences—and created a wonderfully functional complex of terraces, courtyards, and indoor spaces. Pillars and thick walls of carefully fitted stones lend dramatic mass to the structures and reflect a style inspired by California's climate and Franciscan missions. A large arbor supported by stone columns joins two heritage oaks in shading the entryway, as soft music drifts about the courtyard and blends with the pleasing sound of water in nearby fountains.

Inside, visitors can wander through the gift shop stocked with locally produced items, kitchenware, crystal glasses, and gourmet goodies before heading into the impressive tasting area. Just past the exposed stone walls of the foyer, a massive fireplace promises winter warmth, large artworks inspired by the vineyard hang below a row of lofty windows, and a sheer sense of space prevails. In front of a huge, arched window that looks over the demonstration vineyard, stacked glassware glints from behind the triangular concrete bar. Here, wine aficionados may taste a selection of Vina Robles estate wines and sip the winery's Cuvée Collection of signature blends.

Marc Laderriere, vice president of sales, notes that because of the winery's Swiss heritage, its principals embrace a "European approach" that favors food-friendly wines with modest alcohol content and a bright finish. To promote the enjoyment of wine with food, the winery offers a number of wine-and-food pairings. They include a creative pairing of up to six artisan cheeses and special release wines, the Wine and Chocolate Experience featuring locally made truffles, and the Gourmet Lunch Tasting, which begins with a sampling of wines, followed by a wine country lunch.

In 2013 the winery celebrated the opening of the Vina Robles Amphitheatre, a 3,300-seat outdoor venue that ranks among the largest in San Luis Obispo County. Set into an oak-dotted hillside, the boutique amphitheatre hosts such world-class musical acts as Sarah Brightman and Bonnie Raitt, as well as top-tier comedians and local performers. A well-stocked concession area offers wine, craft beer, wood-fired pizzas, salads, and sandwiches during the show. Guests can choose among regular, luxury box, and lawn seats, all within 150 feet of the elegant stage, which features a stacked stone proscenium and state-of-the-art sound system.

VINA ROBLES
3700 Mill Rd.
Paso Robles, CA 93446
805-227-4812
info@vinarobles.com
vinarobles.com

OWNERS: Hans Nef, Hans–R. Michel and families.

LOCATION: 3 miles east of U.S. 101 off Hwy. 46 East.

APPELLATION: Paso Robles.

HOURS: 10 A.M.–5 P.M. daily in winter, 10 A.M.–6 P.M. daily in summer.

TASTINGS: $7 for 5 estate wines. $10 for reserve tasting, including Cuvée Collection.

TOURS: None.

THE WINES: Cabernet Sauvignon, Petit Verdot, Petite Sirah, Sauvignon Blanc, Syrah.

SPECIALTIES: Estate blends such as Red[4] and White[4], Signature, Syrée, Suendero.

WINEMAKER: Kevin Willenborg.

ANNUAL PRODUCTION: 35,000 cases.

OF SPECIAL NOTE: Food-and-wine pairings offered daily. Extensive shop featuring gourmet foods and cookbooks. Deli section with artisan cheeses. Terrace and patio seating.

NEARBY ATTRACTIONS: Barney Schwartz Park (lake, picnic areas); Estrella Warbird Museum (restored military aircraft, memorabilia).

WILD HORSE WINERY

WILD HORSE WINERY
1437 Wild Horse
Winery Ct.
Templeton, CA 93465
805-788-6300
leslie.churchill@
wildhorsewinery.com
wildhorsewinery.com

LOCATION: 10 miles south
of Paso Robles.

APPELLATION: Paso Robles.

HOURS: 11 A.M.–5 P.M. daily.

TASTINGS: $5 for 5 wines.

TOURS: Weekends by
appointment.

THE WINES: Blaufränkisch,
Cabernet Sauvignon,
Chardonnay, Malvasia
Bianca, Merlot, Pinot Noir,
Verdelho, Viognier.

SPECIALTIES: Cheval
Sauvage (Pinot Noir),
Pinot Noir.

WINEMAKER:
Chrissy Wittmann.

ANNUAL PRODUCTION:
200,000 cases.

OF SPECIAL NOTE: Patio
for picnicking. Gift shop
featuring local olive oil,
wine accessories, and other
items. Free organic pro-
duce in season. Heirloom
and Unbridled wines available only in tasting room.

NEARBY ATTRACTIONS:
Barney Schwartz Park
(lake, picnic areas);
Estrella Warbird Museum
(restored military aircraft,
memorabilia).

One of the oldest producers in the Central Coast region, Wild Horse Winery completed its first crush in 1983, the year that Paso Robles became an official appellation. Named for the wild mustangs that once roamed the neighboring hills, it remains a local favorite, renowned for its eclectic portfolio of wines, prolific organic vegetable garden, and Floyd, the resident llama.

Wild Horse chose the eastside of Paso Robles for its vineyard because of the area's low-vigor soils, believing their lean constitution would force the sustainably farmed vineyard to produce grapes with highly concentrated flavors. As an ambitious experiment, forty-five acres were planted with thirty-three varietals, some of them considered unusual even by today's standards. Among the blocks of Cabernet Sauvignon and Blaufränkisch, from which tasting-room-exclusive vintinue to employ the sustainable winery. They brew compost tea the-art water recycling system, behind by the grape presses. trol and are protected from

were heirlooms like Verdelho the winery still produces tages. Vineyard workers conmethods used early on by the to feed the vines, use a state-ofand compost the pomace left Sheep are used for weed concoyotes by Floyd.

The winery and tasting room lie beyond two ranch-style gates and at the end of a long road bordered by vineyards. Leading to the tasting room on the ground floor of a two-story complex is a wooden pergola that bisects a lawn and patio set with tables and chairs. Flower beds edge the grass, and half barrels planted with New Zealand flax and trailing succulents line the shaded path to the tasting room door. An equine theme informs the decor of the intimate room, where Saltillo floor tiles enhance the western flavor. A framed photo of three wild mustangs mirrors the winery's logo horse as it gallops across hats, T-shirts, and wine bottles. Display tables and shelves, some crafted from old wine barrels, offer a diverse assortment of books, wine accessories, nut brittle, and local olive oil. At the white oak tasting bar, visitors can sample selections from wine lists aptly titled Unbridled, the Four Horsemen, and Cheval Sauvage.

Today, the estate vineyard provides about 4 percent of the fruit needed to fuel the facility's extensive varietal program, so every fall winemaker Chrissy Wittmann selects from grapes grown in more than forty Central Coast vineyards, some of which have been supplying Wild Horse Winery since its inception.

WINDWARD VINEYARD

True vignerons, Windward Vineyard's Marc Goldberg and Maggie D'Ambrosia make wine according to the Burgundian model of "monopole": maintaining complete control over their vines, vinifying only estate fruit, and never buying a single grape. In their fifteen-acre vineyard, planted exclusively to Pinot Noir, the duo grows four clones chosen specifically to allow the vineyard "to speak about itself in the glass." Goldberg doesn't fine, filter, or acidulate the wine, a minimalist approach that he feels lets the signature qualities of each vineyard block shine through.

The couple releases one wine featuring honeyed notes of wild and what Goldberg calls "the ish," a fanning out of complex oak. In 2012, after twenty years Goldberg and D'Ambrosia were of the Year by the Paso Robles winery's Pinot Noir.

a year—the estate Monopole strawberries and Bing cherries, Windward peacock-tail fin-flavors dusted with a touch of of meticulous winemaking, named Wine Industry Persons Wine Country Alliance for the

Goldberg, who describes his first sip of Pinot Noir at age seventeen as "magic," makes wine in a traditional style that benefits from twenty years or more of cellaring. He marvels at the fifteen hundred years that it took for Pinot Noir to become Burgundy's king, and regards his own role not as that of a technician but as a "wine shepherd" charged with protecting the integrity of his grapes.

In the late 1960s, over a glass of Champagne, Goldberg met D'Ambrosia, his future wife and business partner, in his hometown of Pittsburgh, Pennsylvania. Both were hospital administrators, and as they relocated as necessary for their jobs, they eventually crossed the country, tasting Pinot Noir along the way. The pair preferred nuanced French vintages to the denser New World offerings, until they sampled a 1976 Hoffman Mountain Ranch Pinot Noir from a vineyard five miles west of Paso Robles. Struck by the balance and beauty of the wine, they embraced the grand challenge of making Burgundian-style Pinot Noir in the United States.

Inspired by the work of Dr. Hoffman and the legendary enologist André Tchelistcheff, who in the late 1960s planted some of the westside's first Pinot Noir, the couple bought a barley farm in the Templeton Gap region west of Paso Robles. They planted their vineyard in 1989, on land bearing conditions similar to those of Hoffman's ranch nearby, and released their first wine in 1993.

Visitors to Windward Vineyard's art-filled tasting room find an atmosphere of cool elegance amid the rural quiet. Tucked behind an ivy-draped lath house, the combination winery/tasting room offers a view of the barrel room and an ideal setting for discovering the magic of Pinot Noir.

WINDWARD VINEYARD
1380 Live Oak Rd.
Paso Robles, CA 93446
805-239-2565
maggie@windward
vineyard.com
windwardvineyard.com

OWNERS: Marc Goldberg, Maggie D'Ambrosia.

LOCATION: 1.5 miles west of U.S. 101, off Hwy. 46 West.

APPELLATION: Paso Robles.

HOURS: 10:30 A.M.–5 P.M. daily.

TASTINGS: $10 for 4 wines.

TOURS: By appointment.

THE WINE: Pinot Noir.

SPECIALTY: Estate-grown Burgundian-style Pinot Noir.

WINEMAKER: Marc Goldberg.

ANNUAL PRODUCTION: 2,000 cases.

OF SPECIAL NOTE: Ivy-covered lath house with vineyard view for picnicking. Artisan cheeses, local salami, and gourmet tapenade available for purchase. Nearly all the wine is sold exclusively through tasting room.

NEARBY ATTRACTION: Paso Robles City Park (site of festivals, summer concerts, farmers market).

CENTRAL COAST WINE VARIETALS

The wineries in this book currently produce the following wines, as well as many unique, proprietary blends. Before you visit a tasting room to sample or purchase a particular wine variety, contact the winery to make sure it is available.

AGLIANICO
Pear Valley Vineyards

ALBARIÑO
Barr Estate Winery
Derby Wine Estates
Opolo Vineyards
PasoPort Wine Company
Pear Valley Vineyards

BARBERA
Castoro Cellars
Eberle Winery
Opolo Vineyards

BLAUFRÄNKISCH
Wild Horse Winery

CABERNET FRANC
Carr Vineyards & Winery
Foley Food & Wine Society
foxen 7200
Grassini Family Vineyards
HammerSky Vineyards
Hearst Ranch Winery
Hearthstone Estate
Justin Vineyards & Winery
Pear Valley Vineyards
Silver Wines

CABERNET SAUVIGNON
Barr Estate Winery
Beckmen Vineyards
Calcareous Vineyard
Castoro Cellars
Costa de Oro Winery
Derby Wine Estates
Eberle Winery
Eos
Foley Food & Wine Society
foxen 7200
Grassini Family Vineyards

Grey Wolf Cellars and Barton
  Vineyards
Halter Ranch Vineyard
HammerSky Vineyards
Hearst Ranch Winery
Hearthstone Estate
J. Lohr Vineyards & Wines
Justin Vineyards & Winery
Laetitia Vineyard & Winery
Opolo Vineyards
PasoPort Wine Company
Pear Valley Vineyards
Penman Springs Vineyard
Pomar Junction Vineyard &
  Winery
Sextant Wines
Silver Wines
Siot and Rotta Winery
SummerWood Winery
Talley Vineyards
Treana and Hope Family Wines
Vina Robles
Wild Horse Winery

CHARBONO
Castoro Cellars
Pear Valley Vineyards

CHARDONNAY
Alma Rosa Winery & Vineyards
Byron
Calcareous Vineyard
Cambria Estate Winery
Castoro Cellars
Chamisal Vineyards
Costa de Oro Winery
D'Alfonso-Curran Wines
Demetria Estate Winery
Eberle Winery
Eos
Fess Parker Winery & Vineyard
Foley Estates Vineyard & Winery
Foley Food & Wine Society

Fox Wine Co.
Foxen
Grey Wolf Cellars and Barton
  Vineyards
Hearst Ranch Winery
J. Lohr Vineyards & Wines
Laetitia Vineyard & Winery
Loring/Cargasacchi Tasting
  Room
Opolo Vineyards
Pali Wine Co.
Pear Valley Vineyards
Pomar Junction Vineyard &
  Winery
Sanford Winery & Vineyards
Sextant Wines
Silver Wines
Siot and Rotta Winery
Talley Vineyards
Treana and Hope Family Wines
Wild Horse Winery
Zaca Mesa Winery & Vineyards

CHENIN BLANC
Castoro Cellars
Foxen
Grey Wolf Cellars and Barton
  Vineyards
Pear Valley Vineyards

CINSAULT
Demetria Estate Winery

COUNOISE
Beckmen Vineyards
Demetria Estate Winery

GEWÜRZTRAMINER
Castoro Cellars
Foley Food & Wine Society

GRENACHE
Beckmen Vineyards
Blair Fox Cellars
Carr Vineyards & Winery
Castoro Cellars
Chamisal Vineyards
D'Alfonso-Curran Wines
Demetria Estate Winery
Foxen
Hearthstone Estate
J. Lohr Vineyards & Wines
Opolo Vineyards
PasoPort Wine Company
Pear Valley Vineyards
Siot and Rotta Winery
SummerWood Winery
Treana and Hope Family Wines
Zaca Mesa Winery & Vineyards

GRENACHE BLANC
Beckmen Vineyards
D'Alfonso-Curran Wines
Demetria Estate Winery
Pomar Junction Vineyard &
    Winery
Silver Wines
Zaca Mesa Winery & Vineyards

MALBEC
Barr Estate Winery
Castoro Cellars
Foley Food & Wine Society
Hearst Ranch Winery
Justin Vineyards & Winery
Opolo Vineyards
Pear Valley Vineyards

MALVASIA BIANCA
Wild Horse Winery

MARSANNE
Beckmen Vineyards
Castoro Cellars
Demetria Estate Winery
Derby Wine Estates
SummerWood Winery
Treana and Hope Family Wines

MERLOT
Carhartt Vineyard
Castoro Cellars
Costa de Oro Winery
D'Alfonso-Curran Wines
Derby Wine Estates
Foley Food & Wine Society
foxen 7200
Grassini Family Vineyards
HammerSky Vineyards
Hearst Ranch Winery
Hitching Post Wines
J. Lohr Vineyards & Wines
Justin Vineyards & Winery
Loring/Cargasacchi Tasting
    Room
Opolo Vineyards
PasoPort Wine Company
Penman Springs Vineyard
Pomar Junction Vineyard &
    Winery

Treana and Hope Family Wines
Wild Horse Winery

MOSCATO
Eos
Foley Food & Wine Society

MOURVÈDRE
Beckmen Vineyards
Demetria Estate Winery
Foxen
Hearthstone Estate
J. Lohr Vineyards & Wines
Opolo Vineyards
Siot and Rotta Winery
Zaca Mesa Winery & Vineyards

MUSCAT BLANC
Pear Valley Vineyards
Penman Springs Vineyard

MUSCAT CANELLI
Castoro Cellars
Eberle Winery
Eos
Opolo Vineyards

NEBBIOLO
D'Alfonso-Curran Wines
Silver Wines

ORANGE MUSCAT
Pear Valley Vineyards

PETIT VERDOT
Barr Estate Winery
Calcareous Vineyard
Castoro Cellars
Foley Food & Wine Society
Grassini Family Vineyards
HammerSky Vineyards
Opolo Vineyards
Penman Springs Vineyard
Vina Robles

PETITE SIRAH
Barr Estate Winery
Blair Fox Cellars
Castoro Cellars
Derby Wine Estates

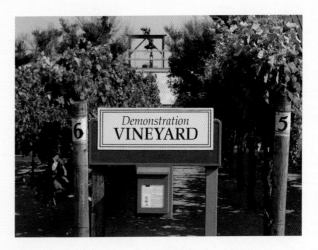

Demonstration VINEYARD

Eos
Foley Food & Wine Society
Hearst Ranch Winery
Hearthstone Estate
J. Lohr Vineyards & Wines
Opolo Vineyards
Pear Valley Vineyards
Penman Springs Vineyard
Siot and Rotta Winery
Vina Robles

PICPOUL BLANC
Demetria Estate Winery

PINOT BLANC
Alma Rosa Winery & Vineyards
Byron
Foley Food & Wine Society

PINOT GRIGIO
Castoro Cellars
Costa de Oro Winery
D'Alfonso-Curran Wines
Loring/Cargasacchi Tasting
    Room
Opolo Vineyards

PINOT GRIS
Alma Rosa Winery & Vineyards
Cambria Estate Winery
Carr Vineyards & Winery
Chamisal Vineyards
Derby Wine Estates
Foley Food & Wine Society
Siot and Rotta Winery

PINOT NOIR
Alma Rosa Winery & Vineyards
Byron
Calcareous Vineyard
Cambria Estate Winery
Carhartt Vineyard
Carr Vineyards & Winery
Castoro Cellars
Chamisal Vineyards

Costa de Oro Winery
D'Alfonso-Curran Wines
Demetria Estate Winery
Derby Wine Estates
Fess Parker Winery & Vineyard
Foley Estates Vineyard & Winery
Foley Food & Wine Society
Fox Wine Co.
Foxen
Hearthstone Estate
Hitching Post Wines
J. Lohr Vineyards & Wines
Laetitia Vineyard & Winery
Loring/Cargasacchi Tasting
    Room
Opolo Vineyards
Pali Wine Co.
PasoPort Wine Company
Pear Valley Vineyards
Pomar Junction Vineyard &
    Winery
Sanford Winery & Vineyards
Sextant Wines
Silver Wines
Talley Vineyards
Wild Horse Winery
Windward Vineyard

PORT AND OTHER FORTIFIED WINES
Eberle Winery
Eos
PasoPort Wine Company
Penman Springs Vineyard

PRIMITIVO
Caliza Winery

RIESLING
Demetria Estate Winery
Fess Parker Winery & Vineyard
Foley Food & Wine Society
J. Lohr Vineyards & Wines
Talley Vineyards

ROSÉ
Barr Estate Winery
Caliza Winery
D'Alfonso-Curran Wines
Eos
Foley Estates Vineyard & Winery
Foley Food & Wine Society
Halter Ranch Vineyard
Hearst Ranch Winery
Hitching Post Wines
Pear Valley Vineyards
Pomar Junction Vineyard & Winery
Siot and Rotta Winery

ROUSSANNE
Calcareous Vineyard
Castoro Cellars
Demetria Estate Winery
Derby Wine Estates
Hearthstone Estate
Opolo Vineyards
Pomar Junction Vineyard & Winery
Siot and Rotta Winery
Treana and Hope Family Wines
Zaca Mesa Winery & Vineyards

SANGIOVESE
Carhartt Vineyard
Carr Vineyards & Winery
D'Alfonso-Curran Wines
Eberle Winery
foxen 7200
Hearthstone Estate
Opolo Vineyards
Silver Wines

SAUVIGNON BLANC
Beckmen Vineyards
Carhartt Vineyard
Carr Vineyards & Winery
Castoro Cellars
Costa de Oro Winery
Eos
Foley Food & Wine Society
Fox Wine Co.
foxen 7200

Grassini Family Vineyards
Grey Wolf Cellars and Barton Vineyards
J. Lohr Vineyards & Wines
Justin Vineyards & Winery
Pear Valley Vineyards
Sanford Winery & Vineyards
Talley Vineyards
Vina Robles

SÉMILLON
Eos

SPARKLING WINE
Castoro Cellars
Laetitia Vineyard & Winery
Pomar Junction Vineyard & Winery

SYRAH
Beckmen Vineyards
Blair Fox Cellars
Calcareous Vineyard
Caliza Winery
Cambria Estate Winery
Carhartt Vineyard
Carr Vineyards & Winery
Castoro Cellars
Chamisal Vineyards
Costa de Oro Winery
Demetria Estate Winery
Derby Wine Estates
Eberle Winery
Eos
Fess Parker Winery & Vineyard
Foley Estates Vineyard & Winery
Foley Food & Wine Society
Foxen
Halter Ranch Vineyard
Hearthstone Estate
Hitching Post Wines
J. Lohr Vineyards & Wines
Justin Vineyards & Winery
Laetitia Vineyard & Winery
Opolo Vineyards
PasoPort Wine Company
Pear Valley Vineyards
Penman Springs Vineyard

Pomar Junction Vineyard & Winery
Silver Wines
Siot and Rotta Winery
SummerWood Winery
Talley Vineyards
Treana and Hope Family Wines
Vina Robles
Zaca Mesa Winery & Vineyards

TEMPRANILLO
Castoro Cellars
Costa de Oro Winery
D'Alfonso-Curran Wines
Demetria Estate Winery
Hearst Ranch Winery
Hearthstone Estate
Opolo Vineyards
PasoPort Wine Company

TOURIGA NACIONAL
PasoPort Wine Company

VALDIGUIÉ
J. Lohr Vineyards & Wines

VERDELHO
Wild Horse Winery

VERMENTINO
Blair Fox Cellars

VIN GRIS
Sanford Winery & Vineyards

VIOGNIER
Beckmen Vineyards
Blair Fox Cellars
Calcareous Vineyard
Caliza Winery
Cambria Estate Winery
Castoro Cellars

Demetria Estate Winery
Derby Wine Estates
Eberle Winery
Fess Parker Winery & Vineyard
Grey Wolf Cellars and Barton Vineyards
Halter Ranch Vineyard
Hearthstone Estate
J. Lohr Vineyards & Wines
Opolo Vineyards
Pear Valley Vineyards
Pomar Junction Vineyard & Winery
Silver Wines
SummerWood Winery
Treana and Hope Family Wines
Wild Horse Winery
Zaca Mesa Winery & Vineyards

ZINFANDEL
Calcareous Vineyard
Carhartt Vineyard
Castoro Cellars
Derby Wine Estates
Eberle Winery
Eos
Foley Food & Wine Society
Grey Wolf Cellars and Barton Vineyards
HammerSky Vineyards
Hearst Ranch Winery
Hearthstone Estate
J. Lohr Vineyards & Wines
Opolo Vineyards
PasoPort Wine Company
Pear Valley Vineyards
Pomar Junction Vineyard & Winery
Sextant Wines
Siot and Rotta Winery
SummerWood Winery
Treana and Hope Family Wines

Wine House Press
127 East Napa Street, Suite E
Sonoma, CA 95476
707-996-1741

Editor and publisher: Tom Silberkleit
Original design: Jennifer Barry Design
Production: Poulson Gluck Design
Copyeditor: Judith Dunham
Cartographer: Ben Pease
Color correction: Eviltron
Artistic development: Lisa Silberkleit
Proofreader: Linda Bouchard

All photographs by Robert Holmes, except the following:
page 17, Deborah Cash; page 33, bottom left, courtesy Winescapes Photography; page 33, bottom right, courtesy Sarah Fox;
page 45, courtesy D'Alfonso-Curran Wines; page 97, courtesy HammerSky Vineyards;
page 102, bottom left, courtesy J. Lohr Vineyards & Wines; page 129, bottom right, courtesy Vina Robles.

Front cover photograph: Opolo Vineyards, Paso Robles
Back cover photographs: top left: Laetitia Vineyard & Winery; top right: Opolo Vineyards;
bottom left: Siot and Rotta Winery; bottom right: Sanford Winery & Vineyards

"What Is an Appellation?," "The Making of Wine," "The Art of Barrel Making," "Modern Stoppers," "The Food and Wine Connection,"
"Reading a Wine Label," and "The Etiquette of Wine Tasting": K. Reka Badger, Cheryl Crabtree, and Marty Olmstead

Printed and bound in China through Imago Sales (USA) Inc.
ISBN-13: 978-0-9853628-2-9

Third Edition

Distributed by Publishers Group West, 1700 4th Street, Berkeley, CA 94710, pgw.com

The publisher has made every effort to ensure the accuracy of the information contained in
The California Directory of Fine Wineries, but can accept no liability for any loss, injury, or inconvenience
sustained by any visitor as a result of any information or recommendation contained in this guide.
Travelers should always call ahead to confirm hours of operation, fees, and other highly variable information.

Always act responsibly when drinking alcoholic beverages by selecting a designated driver or prearranged transportation.

Customized Editions
Wine House Press will print custom editions of this volume for bulk purchase at your request. Personalized covers and
foil-stamped corporate logo imprints can be created in large quantities for special promotions or events, or as premiums.
For more information, contact Custom Imprints, Wine House Press, 127 E. Napa Street, Suite E, Sonoma, CA 95476; 707-996-1741.

Join the Facebook Fan Page: facebook.com/CaliforniaFineWineries
Follow us on Twitter: twitter.com/cafinewineries
Visit our website: CaliforniaFineWineries.com

ACKNOWLEDGMENTS

Creativity, perseverance, integrity, and commitment are fundamental qualities for guaranteeing the success of a project. The artistic and editorial teams who worked on this edition possess these qualities in large measures. My heartfelt thanks go to K. Reka Badger, Cheryl Crabtree, and Daniel Mangin, writers; Robert Holmes, photographer; Judith Dunham, copyeditor; Linda Bouchard, proofreader; Poulson Gluck Design, production; Scott Runcorn, color correction; Ben Pease, cartographer; and Linda Siemer, administration.

In addition, I am grateful for the invaluable counsel and encouragement of Danny Biederman; Fran Clow; Morgan McLaughlin; Christopher Taranto; my esteemed parents— Estelle Silberkleit and William Silberkleit; and the scores of readers and winery enthusiasts who have contacted me over the past decade to say how much they enjoy this book series.

I also extend my deepest appreciation to Victor Popp and the staff of La Quinta Inn and Suites of Paso Robles, California, as well as former assistant manager Paul Gaines and the staff of the Hampton Inn & Suites of San Luis Obispo, for their superb hospitality and enthusiastic support of this project. Special thanks also go to Maurice Boyd of Fess Parker's Santa Barbara County Wine Center for lending critical logistic assistance.

And finally, for her love and creative input, as well as for enduring work-filled weekends and midnight deadlines, my gratitude and affection go to Lisa Silberkleit.

— Tom Silberkleit

OTHER BOOKS BY WINE HOUSE PRESS

The California Directory of Fine Wineries — Northern Region
Napa • Sonoma • Mendocino

Also available in e-book format for iPad, Kindle, Kobo, Nook and other tablets.